THE PAINLESS
STOP SMOKING CURE

ISBN: 1453674160
ISBN-13: 9781453674161
LCCN: 2010910574

THE PAINLESS
STOP SMOKING CURE
How EVERYBODY can stop smoking, including YOU!

ᕬ

Eric Eraly

Copyright 2010
www.PainlessStopSmokingCure.com

Preface

Dear Friend,

I smoked for more than twenty years. Occasionally I would think about quitting smoking, but I always found an excuse. I would say, "I can quit when I need to; I'm not like everyone else." On top of this, I didn't want to quit. I thought I liked it, and I felt good doing it.

They were all excuses and self-betrayal. Looking back at the situation, it shows how a human can fool himself so well, for so long. Deep down in my heart, I was afraid. I was afraid to fail, afraid to get hurt, afraid that it would take effort, afraid that I would put on weight. I was afraid that I would miss something, afraid to admit that I was not in control.

First, let me congratulate you on buying this book. It's your first step to your Final Liberation. You have shown that you want to change your current situation. You have shown that you really want to get rid of those cigarettes.

And…there is a good chance that you are afraid. Maybe a little, maybe a little bit more. It's OK, and it's quite normal. Let me try to relax you by telling you a story. I smoked about one million cigarettes in my life. In the last fifteen years, I smoked between eighty and one hundred cigarettes a day.

That was until I found out that quitting was the easiest thing I could do in my entire life. I have always been terribly afraid to stop smoking, and the moment I experienced my Final Liberation, I knew it was the easiest thing to do. It didn't take any effort, there were no so-called withdrawal pains, and I didn't miss a thing. It was, on the contrary, a big celebration.

I imagine you have some questions when you read these words, as I did for so many years. I get all the pleasure in you reading this book. Yes, you read that right. I take 100 percent of the credit for myself. I am the only person who stopped smoking. I have only myself to congratulate for this. When you have finished this book and smoked your last cigarette, you will owe this only to yourself! You will be the only one who has liberated yourself from cigarettes, nobody else.

You are probably thinking, "Yeah, but I bought this book so that someone could help me stop smoking." This book will be your guide on your adventure to your Final Liberation. When you finally arrive there, it's not the guide, but *you*, who went through the whole adventure. You took every single step. You discovered that quitting is the easiest thing to do.

I got the energy to write this book from the relief and discovery that quitting smoking is the easiest thing for a smoker to do. This discovery changed my entire life. Through this book, I would like to contribute to the community by sharing this idea with as many smokers as possible.

Millions of smokers have quit in a heartbeat without any effort, without any stress, without any withdrawal pains. It's just a pity they were never able to tell you how they actually did it. It just happened. They quit and that was it. They couldn't describe how they did it. In this book, you'll find the thought process that all these smokers probably went through in order to reach their Final Liberation. I have been lucky because I took notes of the different steps I followed to free myself. I'm very happy that I can share these steps with you.

I'm convinced that everybody who follows these steps will be able to stop smoking in a very easy, relaxed, and comfortable way.

Don't worry; there is not one single hair on my head that doubts your ability to succeed. You'll succeed, I promise. I just want to ensure that you are making an investment where you can't lose!

I know that you'll be a *free*, happy nonsmoker in a while.

So, let's get started! Start reading the book in an easy, relaxed way. The first time you read the book, try to do so quickly. Where asked, start doing the easy-to-follow steps or instructions. Feel free to smoke while reading the book.

You are about to begin one of the greatest adventures of your entire life; the adventure to your Final Liberation!

All the best,

Eric Eraly

Contents

1. My first cigarette was a cigar!

My first contact with cigarettes was at the age of five. I opened the big antique closet that my parents had in the living room and took out a big cigar. I ran up to my room, opened the window, and "enjoyed" my first cigar. It was an awful experience, and I coughed up my lungs.

I spent the next two days walking from my bed to the bathroom and back. It was the most awful, disgusting experience ever! So, after that experience, I "quit" for a couple of years. The reasons were obvious. First, I had a very bad first experience; my body suffered for quite a while. Second, I didn't get my parents' permission to smoke, obviously, since I was only five. Third, they started hiding the key to the closet a lot better than before.

By the time I was eleven years old, I fell for the temptation of "becoming a real man." I wanted to be cool and belong to the "in" gang. It happened when I was at boarding school. It was a school run by Jesuits, who, as you'll later see, played quite a considerable role in my smoking education. Spending the first night with three other pupils, all around eleven years old, and sharing a room was quite a lot of fun. It was a new experience for all of us, as we got to know each other and found out who already smoked. Marc was one of those guys who didn't just talk about having done it, he actually smoked, and he showed us his cigarettes, Blue Belga with a filter.

The next morning, after introductions to the class and teacher, a few of us escaped into the woods. There we would meet and smoke. The trip was an experience in itself; we felt like we were in a movie, and it was a little bit scary. There was always a potential risk of being caught, but what a challenge! I guess we were in a group of six or seven kids, hiding behind some big bushes, while Marc and Rob were distributing the cigarettes and then lighting them. It didn't take much to convince me to go along with them, because I wanted to be a part of it; I wanted to belong to the group. Just that sensation was a big adventure that I didn't want to miss.

Anyway, at eleven years old, I had another nicotine stick in my mouth, and I was about to experience the "great sensation" and taste of it. Well, it was even worse than that cigar I smoked when I was five! After the first puff, I immediately started coughing, and it seemed that my whole head started to spin around. From time to time, I felt as if I was going to faint. I was dizzy, and I saw my colleagues floating and turning around as I collapsed on the sand under the bushes.

Some of the guys started to laugh at me. "A-ha, you can't stand the smoke. Whoa, you pussy." "You're not a real guy." "You're so soft." I didn't want to admit I was failing and tried to show them the real me by taking another large puff. The result wasn't any better, and the taste was absolutely awful. It felt as though the smoke was slowly penetrating my throat, my lungs, and my stomach. I felt sick. My legs and arms felt heavy, my knees couldn't keep my body up, and so I stayed lying on the ground, just turning my head. My eyes were wide open, so I could see what was happening. This was the only sure thing that I experienced; I could still see what was going on around me. It was small consolation to notice that I wasn't the only person suffering from this experience.

As we were in a group of "grown-up" kids, nobody wanted to show his weakness; just the contrary. Besides, everybody wanted to belong to the group, be one of those big guys who dared to escape to the woods and smoke without permission.

We all survived our first nicotine experience, as well as our trip back to the schoolyard. Such a trip was not without danger. The school kept us under close surveillance, and if the instructors had caught us, it would have cost us our school careers. Not to mention how our parents would have reacted once they found out about it.

Back in school, the news about our group spread like wildfire. We were the kids from the gang that dared to break the rules. We were famous! Unbelievable, we were famous and admired by our colleagues. Some of them joined our club, others were afraid, but the majority thought what we did was cool. The feeling of being famous, belonging to the group, and doing the forbidden things gave me such a kick that I kept on escaping and smoking with the other guys.

Every Friday afternoon, a big school bus took us back home. It was a one-and-a-half-hour drive from school to my parents' house. Marc was also on my bus, as he lived a few villages further on. The bus had hardly left the grounds of school before we started smoking. Another stimulating factor was that there were girls on our bus. They came from a neighboring boarding school for girls that had an agreement with our school concerning traveling from and to school on Sundays and Fridays.

Smoking and doing other forbidden things was the right thing to do in order to impress the girls. The girls didn't say so, but we just knew; we could read their minds! We were the cowboys of their dreams! I'm not familiar with your story, but I would really like to know how nicotine trapped you. You can always send me your story by mail or e-mail. No matter what the details of your story are, chances are that you can find some similarities with my story.

Maybe you started smoking at quite a young age because you wanted to belong to a group, to be with the big boys in your school. Maybe you did it because you wanted to impress the girls. Maybe you started smoking because you had a big brother or sister that smoked, and you thought it looked cool to have a cigarette in your mouth. Maybe you started to impress your boyfriend.

On the other hand, maybe you started because you wanted to keep your stress or your weight under control. Others started smoking because their best friends convinced them. Advertisements on television or at sports events depicted our heroes with cigarettes in their mouths. Movies showed our favorite actors or actresses relaxing with a delicious cigarette. These are some of the many things that might have pushed you to smoke that very first cigarette.

Maybe you only started smoking as an adult. You went through a difficult period, you had a lot of stress, you felt desperate, you lost a loved one, you felt overwhelmed, and then somebody offered you a cigarette. The rest is history. No matter how you actually started smoking, it has always been a struggle in your mind whether you should or shouldn't do it. In fact, our minds are hearing conflicting messages from the day we are born. Very often, we are not aware of this internal struggle.

Imagine the scene. A newborn visited by his grandfather. Hanging over the baby with a fat cigar in his mouth, the mother yells at him to take that disgusting cigar away from the baby. As far as the baby is concerned, it stinks and isn't very pleasant. If only a mother's advice could stay in our minds forever. While growing up, the young child sees his grandfather on many occasions, and he always has the cigar. Now the child gets a completely different picture of the cigar. He is told it's for grown-ups who have enough money to afford it. Or the child hears the grandfather sharing how he enjoys a good cigar after lunch.

There are also negative signals. The child sees the grandfather coughing in the morning, or hears from teachers at school how bad and unhealthy smoking is. You can get cancer from it. The mind gets very confused. On television, you hear your own hero say how wonderful a cigarette tastes. You see your favorite actor almost have a nervous breakdown, then get back to normal after having a nice puff.

The mind of the young person has no idea who is right and who is wrong. This conflicting stream of information goes on and on. On one side, you hear and see part of the population telling you that smoking is bad, ugly, and unhealthy. The other half tells you exactly the opposite. Smoking is cool, it's good for stress and boredom, it tastes great, it makes you feel free, your performance increases. No matter which party is right, you end up as a confused young adolescent.

What is a common reaction for a young and confused adolescent? *Try it out!* Therefore, the next step is that you actually try it; you put to the test everything that people have told you. You are going to experiment to see which media, people, and sources are right and which are wrong. Something in you doesn't believe that your hero can be wrong.

Most first experiences with a cigarette are similar. It's a disgusting experience. I have to admit right away that I've met several people who claim that their first cigarette really tasted good! In most cases, it was a person who started smoking as an adult. I'm not sure if this has an influence, but I still find it hard to believe that a first cigarette tastes good. For most of you, the first cigarette wasn't a great experience. It tasted bad and dull; it made you cough and probably made you a little dizzy. If this was all there was to say about smoking, then you would easily be able to distinguish the right group from the wrong one. It would be so simple if nicotine were just a simple test like that.

However, it's not.

First, you have awakened the balloon in your body. The balloon has always been there, but as long as it's not fed externally with nicotine, it remains asleep. Second, you become more confused. You think about your heroes; how can they be so wrong? All those people who've told you that it tastes so wonderful. You think you must be doing something completely wrong, and you think you have to try it again. And that's exactly what you do. You light another cigarette to prove to yourself that you were wrong. If you hadn't done that, you wouldn't be reading this book right now.

So, you tried it a second time, a third time, and so on. And every time, you were feeding the nicotine balloon and providing it with more energy and power to fight back. In the meanwhile, your body gradually became accustomed to the ugly taste of cigarettes and the consequences of inhaling smoke into your lungs. You became a victim of the peer control of your immediate social circle. Your friends smoked and encouraged you to do the same, you gained status in the group, and you got caught up in the forbidden factor. Suddenly you were no longer confused; smoking was cool! You became a convinced smoker! Congratulations!

Most of you are familiar with the negative reaction of some people to your decision to start smoking. Most certainly, they, meaning primarily your parents and teachers, would have forbidden you to smoke. Of course, that would depend on the age you took up smoking. However, even if you started smoking at a later point in your life, I guess you didn't receive too much positive feedback concerning your new habit, did you?

The fact that something is forbidden makes it even more exciting, especially when your parents and schools forbid it. I remember how exciting it was to smuggle cigarettes into my parents' home and then to decide how and where to hide them! I found a perfect solution.

One week I came home from my boarding school with at least fifty empty boxes of Marlboro. I told my parents and sister that I wanted to collect everything from Marlboro. Nobody was surprised, since I was a big fan of the McLaren Formula 1 team, and at that time their cars were covered with Marlboro advertisements. So I placed the empty boxes in an old unused chimney in my room. One of those fifty boxes would be a full box of cigarettes; the rest would be empty.

I knew which the good box was, and I didn't expect my mother to open those fifty boxes to look for a full one. The collection kept growing from that moment on. In the beginning, my sister was a big supporter of my Marlboro collection. In the end, the collection grew to about three thousand boxes, big posters, every possible ashtray, stickers, etc. It became a mini museum of Marlboro. To this day, nothing has changed in my room at my parents' place.

Another trick I used was the chocolate trick. Someone from school told me that after smoking, I should eat a piece of dark chocolate to get rid of the smell of cigarettes. So before I got off the school bus, I ate a piece of chocolate. Sometimes my mother remarked that I smelled heavily of cigarettes, to which I replied that I had sat next to a person who was smoking. The chocolate proved helpful, but only as far as my breath was concerned. It had no effect on my clothes!

In school, we were very inventive when hiding and smoking our cigarettes. During the short breaks during the day, the smokers went for a smoke, and the favorite place was the bathroom. As a result, there were usually three or four of us standing in one small stall and smoking. The teachers, who had to keep an eye on us during those breaks, weren't stupid, so they checked the bathrooms by looking under the doors and counting the number of feet they could see. Therefore, one person sat on the bowl and three others stood on its sides. It was a funny sight.

Another problem we faced was the smoke itself. Four cigarettes in such a small room meant that the smoke left a visible trace. We kept waving our cigarettes from left to right in order to disperse the smoke. The smoke we inhaled was kept in as long as possible and then blown out against our shirts.

Once we finished our cigarettes, we had to get out of the bathroom. Very often the teachers were standing outside; counting how many people came out of one single stall. After a while, they knew who the heavy smokers were and just made jokes without giving us any real punishment. It was because of all these funny stories that I continued to find smoking so exciting! And that was one of the reasons I kept smoking. At least, that's what I thought.

Even though cigarettes don't taste good in the beginning, you keep going because you like things that are associated with it. You start to enjoy the kick you get from smoking, the emotional kick against your school, teachers, parents, etc. You are dragged into a film where they are the bad guys and you are the hero who has to escape from all their attempts to catch you. And it's a really exciting movie! So, the bad taste of the cigarette is largely compensated for by the excitement and adrenaline you experience while having your forbidden cigarette.

When you read these examples, it might be that you recognize yourself. However, it's also possible that this isn't your story at all. Maybe you started to smoke at a much older age and you really can't imagine these boy-scout stories. When this is the case, another question arises, namely, is there an age at which starting to smoke seems to be completely crazy? I guess the answer to this question is no. The reason is because you actually don't decide to become a smoker. We will come back to this later on.

Let's try to go back to that moment just before you tried your first cigarette. Do you still remember that moment? Can you remember how you felt at that specific time? For some of you it will be possible; for others that experience is too far away. Allow me to share the following idea with you: whether you can remember it or not, it was the last time you truly enjoyed the feeling of freedom. I have just one question for you: "What were you missing in your life just before you smoked that first cigarette?" Have you ever asked yourself that question? Can you answer it?

You might wonder why I'm asking this question. I want you to start a thinking process about your smoking habits that you'll develop and build up while reading this book. Nothing more, nothing less. I'm not here to brainwash you regarding smoking and how bad it is. No, I'll leave that up to you. You are the only person who can make such judgment calls for yourself. I only want to give you the path, a way or guideline that you can follow as you proceed with this book. I want to tell you that you'll be confronted from time to time. It will mostly be confrontations with yourself. These are not always as nice as you might expect them to be. Be prepared!

However, if you are open to the information that will be provided and you are honestly committed to start this thinking process, I guar-

antee, you'll enter on a long lasting journey to your Final Liberation!
And I promise you it will be a smooth, easy journey, as long as you
keep using your powerful mind.

2. What are you afraid of and why?

One of the major reasons people keep smoking is because they are afraid to quit. It is usually an underlying reason most people are not consciously aware of. Just think about the following statement: If I were to tell you right now, that it's over, that you would never, ever be allowed to smoke another cigarette, how would you feel? Are you afraid? Do you feel frightened? Do you have butterflies in your stomach?

How can I know how you feel? Simple: most smokers feel this way. There are several common fears for smokers. I think one of the biggest fears is the fear of not succeeding. You are afraid to fail. Another fear is the fear of going through misery and sacrifice. You are also afraid of not being able to enjoy life fully once you have quit. You are afraid of having to cope at social events without cigarettes.

Finally, you are afraid that you'll miss many joyful things once you have stopped smoking. Because smokers have all these fears, it's difficult to connect with them on the subject of quitting. They are so afraid of this event that they exclude everything that could even remind them of it. They even deny it.

As a smoker, you smoke a lot of cigarettes when you feel fear—when you are afraid of deadlines, when you are afraid of losing your job, when you are afraid of a rejection, etc. So, when I tell you that smoking is bad, that you can get cancer from it, that they might have to cut off your legs, that you are killing yourself, most likely you'll become afraid and you'll want a cigarette. In such a condition, your mind is not open to listening, not open to ways to stop smoking.

Why is it that you are so afraid of just the thought of quitting?

Why are you so afraid?

What are your feelings based upon?

To answer these questions we should look at the basis of fear or the basis of our behavior in general. There is one single driving force for everything we do. Everything human beings do, they do for a reason. This reason or driving force is called the pleasure-pain principle. It states that everything we do, we do either because we want to avoid pain or because we have a strong desire to gain pleasure. It's important that you understand the principle and its consequences.

If everything you do, you do either to avoid pain or to gain pleasure, then why do you still smoke? Everybody knows the painful side effects of smoking. You know that you are killing yourself. You know that by smoking you increase your chances of getting cancer, etc. So, if this principle makes sense, you should quit immediately, right? Well, there is also the other side. This side contains all the illusions, all the beliefs that you have created in your mind about the pleasures of smoking. The basic reason why you still smoke is that you actually link more pain to quitting today than putting it off for a while. You feel more attracted to the pleasures of smoking than to the pain you might feel in twenty years.

On the other hand, you know deep down that you want to quit; you know that you want to free yourself from this nicotine addiction. You feel frustrated, you feel overwhelmed from time to time, and you feel angry with yourself because you know you should take action. However, you don't do anything. You don't try to change your behavior because of a deeper, underlying cause. Once you understand the cause and therefore the reason why you smoke, you'll be able to remove the cause and thus stop smoking.

The first step in changing anything is to understand the true power of the pain-pleasure principle. Think back about some decisions you have made recently. Why did you make those decisions? Why did you do certain things, and why didn't you do the other ones? When you look closely, you'll realize that these things happened because you thought that doing or deciding on a particular thing would give you more pleasure and less pain.

Most of our decisions are short term. Will it mean pleasure in the short term? However, often things that mean pleasure in the short term mean pain in the long term. Just think about the phenomenon of procrastination. At a certain moment, it's much more pleasurable not to take any action. Later on, when it's almost too late, you find yourself in the middle of a painful situation, which forces you to take action at once.

It's the same with smoking. Most smokers think in the short term and are afraid to look at things in the long term. Why are they afraid to look further? Deep down, they know the long-term results of their actions. That is why they focus on the short term, the present. That means pleasure.

To stop smoking means pain when compared to smoking a cigarette. At least that is the idea that a smoker has. So where does this idea come from? It's not the actual pain that drives us, but the fear that something will cause pain. In addition, it's not actual pleasure that drives us, but our belief, our sense of certainty, that taking a certain action will lead to pleasure. This is how we arrive at fear and beliefs.

Fear is a belief. It's a sense of certainty about something. It's a belief that something or someone will cause us pain. You'll see in another chapter the different beliefs we have about smoking. For now, it's enough that you understand where your fear is coming from and how it's created.

As you saw at the beginning of this chapter, there are quite a lot of fears we have about smoking. So, where do they come from? Why do you associate so much pain with these things that they become your fears? Why are you so afraid of quitting? What holds you back from quitting smoking now? Why are you afraid of withdrawal symptoms? Why do you fear you won't succeed?

Unless you have tried to quit before, it's not possible that those beliefs of fear have been created through your own experience, right? Moreover, even if you have tried to quit and it didn't work out, did all those fears appear at once?

Alternatively, do you think there might be something else that has formed those beliefs in your mind? You'll find out that most of your fears, most of your beliefs and illusions, are created by brainwashing about smoking, created by society, other smokers, and also nonsmokers.

Once you understand where your beliefs come from, you can start to analyze them. You can start evaluating them from an objective point of view. Notice that you are the only person who can do this!

A book like this can only guide you through these beliefs. The person who actually evaluates these beliefs and feels certainty about them is you! That is exactly what you are going to do throughout this book. You are going to find out what beliefs about smoking you have. You are going to discover whether these beliefs are true beliefs or whether they are just illusions.

Once you have done this analysis, you are going to analyze the reasons you smoke. You and I are not going to waste our time looking for the reasons why you should stop smoking. You know these, and they are not going to help you. You and I are going to remove all the reasons you smoke.

You are going to free yourself from all the obligations you feel towards smoking. You are going to free yourself from the desire to smoke a cigarette. By accomplishing this, you are going to reach a tremendous state of freedom and joy. Lust for life will become your new motto! You are going to understand that there is absolutely nothing to be afraid of when it comes to quitting smoking. You are going to discover that all the fears you have are just illusions. The moment you'll be a nonsmoker, you'll fully agree with this. For now, I leave you with a thought to open your mind.

"Do the thing you are afraid to do, and the death of fear is certain."

Ralph Waldo Emerson

It's also important that you are a critical reader of this book. I want to ask you to be critical not only of the words you read, but also the thoughts you have and the new thoughts you are going to create. The fact that you are reading this book means that there is something in you, no matter how small, that wants to stop smoking. Your success will mainly depend on your approach towards this book. If you are willing to deeply analyze and understand what you are going to read, your success is guaranteed.

If you have the intention of going quickly through it and retaining your own thoughts, I would advise you not to buy the book. It won't work. It won't be able to help you. On top of this, you won't be able to help yourself, because that's what it's all about. If you have already bought the book, or received it, don't read it if this is your state of mind; it will be a waste of time. Therefore, if you want to continue reading this book, having an open and critical mind is essential. Otherwise, you'd better stop right now. Allow me to give you some general suggestions to keep in mind while you are going through this book.

1. Accept the thought that there is nothing to fear after you stop smoking.

2. Be a critical reader. Be critical of the words you read and the thoughts you have right now.

3. Feel free to smoke as you please. When your Final Liberation comes, you'll feel it, and you'll become a nonsmoker even before extinguishing your last cigarette.

Don't force your behavior. Let yourself be guided by your thoughts. You'll know when the moment has come. I will show you how and when to smoke your last cigarette. Yes, exciting, isn't it?

4. While reading this book and applying the Painless Stop Smoking Cure, feel relaxed and enjoy the moment. You'll discover that there is absolutely nothing to feel stressed about. There is nothing to be afraid of. You are about to become, in a short while, a free and happy nonsmoker, and this will be one of the best moments you'll ever experience in your entire life. Guaranteed!

❦

3. Yes, you have a drug addiction!

When you want to improve a situation, no matter what kind of situation you are dealing with, it's very important to understand precisely what kind of situation you are in. What type of smoker are you?

There are many types of smokers. Maybe you are a chain smoker. Or are you a party smoker? Or maybe a control freak smoker? I don't know, and frankly, I'm not really interested in knowing what type of a smoker you are. What is more important is that *you know* what type of smoker you are. Do you smoke first thing in the morning when you wake up? Do you smoke every time you get into your car? Do you smoke your first cigarette only after 5 p.m.?

Have you figured it out? Now you might be wondering what this is all about. Will information about what type of a smoker you are determine whether you can quit easily or not? Or maybe you won't quit at all. What is going through your mind at the moment? What are you really thinking of at this very instant while reading these words?

Have you captured your thoughts? Fine. Now, please let these thoughts go and promise yourself that you'll never have these thoughts again. Why? Because these thoughts are limiting you on your way to freedom. As I told you earlier, it's not important for me to know what you are thinking when you try to put yourself into one of the smoker categories. It's only important for you to know.

Whatever the thought might be, it's a limiting one. I'll give you just a few possibilities. When you are a chain smoker, puffing more than one hundred cigarettes a day, you might be thinking that you'll never be able to quit, and certainly not without suffering. When you are an occasional smoker who only smokes at parties, you might be telling yourself that your way of smoking is not so bad. After all, you smoke very little, and you are fully in control of your smoking habit. At least that's what you think. In both cases, these are limiting thoughts that stop you from going further in the process to Final Liberation.

What is important to consider? What do you have to understand about your situation in order to keep moving forward? Whether you are a heavy smoker or a light smoker, whether you believe it's a bad habit or a habit you are in control of, it's vital to understand and realize that smoking is not a bad habit! It's not a "habit." It's an *addiction!* Clear and simple. This might sound rude to you, but that's the way it is. Smoking is an addiction, and, yes, you have a drug addiction!

Are you still with me? Good. This is something you must realize and agree with. You have to recognize that you have a drug addiction. As long as you don't admit it to yourself, there is no solution for you. It was a real eye opener I had to accept. I'm not saying that you *are* a drug addict; I only say that you have a drug addiction. The difference is that in the first phrase, "drug addict," you would have to deal with a done situation. In the second phrase, "you have a drug addiction," you are in a situation that you want to change. You suffer from this addiction and you want to get rid of it.

There is some good logic in understanding why smokers and non-smokers want to believe that smoking is just a bad habit. First, we have many habits in our lives, good habits and bad ones. If smoking were just a bad habit, it would be so easy to quit! I wouldn't have to write this book. You could quit just like that! We break good and bad habits every single day. The main reason we believe smoking is a bad habit is that we are brainwashed by society telling us so.

Because we believe that smoking is a bad habit and because we believe that it's difficult to break bad habits, we find it difficult to quit. Do you follow this? Why is it, then, so difficult to stop smoking? Well, first of all, it's very easy to quit—that's the purpose of this whole book. But the reason is because smoking is an addiction to one of the most refined drugs we know, nicotine!

As long as you believe that smoking is just a bad habit, you'll continue to find it difficult to quit. Once you understand it's an addiction, it becomes easy. Of course, nobody likes to admit to being an addict. It sounds pretty lousy and weak to admit to your friends and family that you are an addict, a drug addict. It sounds much better to say, "Well, all of us have our bad habits; mine is smoking." Or you brush off the idea that you are addicted by claiming you are fully in control of your smoking habit.

Telling your wife that you are an addict is not easy. It's even more difficult to admit it to yourself! I remember how I pretended for years and years that I wasn't an addict. I really did! Smoking over one hundred cigarettes a day, I was still claiming that I was smoking because I wanted to and that I was fully in control. I proudly told my friends I could smoke three packs in one night and then refrain from smoking for six hours the next day because I visited my parents, where of course I couldn't smoke.

So, if I really wanted, I could quit in a split second. I was in control, and at that moment in my life I wanted to smoke. The worst thing was that I was not only telling these stupid lies to my friends and family, but also to myself! As long as I was telling these lies to myself, how could I ever quit? I had to be honest with myself. I had to tell myself the truth. Why did I smoke? How did it happen?

That brings me to a point around which I believe a lot of brainwashing and mistakes are associated. When did you make the decision to become a smoker? When was it? Do you remember the place, the specific moment? Silly question? Just think about it; did you ever consciously choose to become a smoker?

Unbelievable, isn't it? Personally, I can't believe that there is one smoker in the world who consciously wanted to become a smoker. It's something you grow into because of all the traps that are set for you. The nicotine trap, the society trap, the habit trap. Before you know it, your body is addicted to the nicotine and you become an addict. You didn't choose to become a smoker. It just happens in the process.

Of course, you shouldn't use that argument to feel sorry for or excuse yourself. On the contrary, it should give you even more reasons to free yourself from a situation and condition you never wanted to be in. You didn't choose to become a smoker, but you can and will choose to become a nonsmoker!

The fact that you have admitted to yourself and others in your close circle that you have a drug addiction is a very important step forward. From now on, you know where you stand. This is important, because without knowing it you can never be sure if you have made any progress.

The other major advantage is the fact that you can start looking for the proper tools to fix the situation. As long as you believe it's just a bad habit or something you choose to do yourself, you're likely to look for solutions in that specific field. As you saw earlier, the fact that you believe smoking is just a bad habit makes quitting smoking much more difficult. That is because you know that it's difficult to break bad habits.

The fact that you believe this makes smoking your top bad-habit example. Unless you admit what you honestly know, namely that you are a drug addict, a *nicotine* addict, it's a vicious circle which you won't escape.

The beautiful thing in admitting this is that now you can choose to set yourself free and become a free person again. You can now take the necessary steps to go back to that moment before you became a smoker.

By the time you know what the best moment is to set yourself free, you'll already be in a completely different state, in which you'll no longer desire a cigarette. Before you achieve this wonderful moment, it's important that you understand how you are brainwashed into smoking and how you can control it.

ॐ

4. The brainwashing

When you go back to the time you started smoking, what are the first thoughts that come to your mind? Are these positive or negative thoughts? Maybe both? Let me share with you how I see it and how I've experienced it throughout my life.

I believe you are confronted with at least two groups: overall society and smoking society. In overall society, you have been confronted since childhood with advertising about smoking telling you how cool it is. Adults told you how smoking helped them to relax and concentrate better. On other occasions, you heard people say that smoking helped them to lose weight. When you went to the movies, you saw all your heroes smoking cigarettes and looking cool. They smoked a cigarette when something exciting was about to happen or after they did a heroic act.

If you were to believe the tobacco advertisements, smoking would make you more assertive and glamorous, help you to control your weight, add excitement to your life, give you more sex appeal and more romance, and even make you sportier. Can you imagine!

When you watch a movie where somebody is executed, what is his or her last wish? A cigarette! The heavily wounded soldier gets a cigarette as relief in a war movie. All this information penetrates unconsciously into our brains. This is one category of heterosuggestion society tells us about smoking. A heterosuggestion is simply a suggestion coming from someone other than oneself.

Another category of society, which grows every day, tells you that smoking is bad. It's bad for your health, dangerous for pregnant women, and you can get cancer from it. You hear about absurd trials where cigarette companies are sued for billions of dollars. You see more and more places where smoking is forbidden: public places, airplanes, trains, bars, cities.

The message is clear; smoking is very bad and dangerous for your health. Smoking is antisocial. It will diminish your chances of getting a job, it's forbidden in so many places, etc. That's the second category of heterosuggestions you hear and experience about smoking.

That's a lot contradictory information, isn't it? Imagine you are twelve years old and your parents smoke. In the morning, you see your father having breakfast. After breakfast, he drinks his cup of coffee, lights a cigarette, and says, "Hmmm, this tastes so good. It will be a great day today, son. Good luck at school." Then you arrive at school, where you see some of your friends hiding in the bathroom, smoking.

When you enter the school building, you see a big sign telling you smoking is not allowed, and you see giant posters informing you that smoking kills. You have biology this morning, and the teacher begins a lesson on smoking, the causes of lung cancer, and its consequences.

All this information is penetrating your mind on a continuous basis. This is very confusing, even for the brightest minds. Even if you are an older man or woman, the information is contradictory and penetrates your mind from the day you are born. The tobacco industry makes sure it has appropriate commercials for all age groups and sexes. It makes clear differences between, for example, male and female commercials.

Over the last couple of years, there have been visible changes in advertising trends, which focus more on the female audience. The reason for this is quite simple. Tobacco companies noticed that more and more men are quitting, and they want to keep their market share. So, they are looking for new markets, and women seem to be a very attractive and successful target.

It's a pity that they play on the weak points of their future customers to seduce them. Many advertisements clearly imply that smoking keeps your weight under control or even makes you lose weight! That way it's easier to attract more clients. Once these messages have penetrated into the minds of hundred of thousands of women, it becomes much more difficult for them to quit. More on this particular topic will be discussed later.

Let's now continue with the contradictory messages or suggestions you receive from our society on a daily basis. It's important to realize that these suggestions are a part of your daily life. This means that you don't actually hear them in a conscious way. These contradictory suggestions have become a part of your general belief system. This makes this society brainwashing even stronger and more powerful.

These contradicting suggestions are a danger and one of the main reasons why it's so difficult to stop smoking. It's also the main reason why you actually started smoking in the beginning. I'll explain why later.

Let's now have a look at who has provided you with suggestions about cigarettes and how you are brainwashed by the smokers' society. Most of us started smoking under some kind of social pressure. This social pressure came from a group of people, friends or family, who were smoking at the moment when you reached for your first cigarette. When you are a young smoker, you probably started smoking in order to belong to a group, feel cool, feel like one of your heroes, feel more charming, or lose weight.

If you were older, you probably started due to a stressful situation—a relationship that ended, a difficult exam or a new job, even a baby in the family. Perhaps you wanted to do something exciting, you wanted to feel more alive, or you needed to concentrate on something, and then you were offered a cigarette.

Just in this variety of reasons, you can find contradictions. Smoking to concentrate and smoking to alleviate boredom, smoking in stress situations and smoking when relaxed. You hear them tell you how tasty a cigarette is after dinner. How they light a cigarette first thing in the morning and how they enjoy it. How they have a puff when they have to think and concentrate, how a cigarette helps them to get fantastic ideas, how they have seduced a partner by blowing smoke in their face!

Unbelievable, isn't it?

You hear all the good things about smoking from those people who know them—smokers.

Moreover, and this makes the cigarette trap complete, you also hear many warnings from smokers, which are meant to discourage you from starting smoking. They tell you about the downside of smoking. It will destroy your health, cost a lot of money, limit your social freedom, make you hooked for life, and so on.

When it comes to quitting smoking, the stories you hear are clear. Quitting is very difficult and you suffer doing it. It's impossible to quit. It's the hardest thing to do if you smoke more than a pack a day.

Without medical help, you can never quit. Even if you quit, you'll restart one day. Your body will shake because it needs nicotine. You'll become angry with friends and family. You'll have problems concentrating and you'll finally start smoking again. You'll hear from people who have tried a number of times and failed every time. Others have used all the pills and patches available and still smoke a pack a day.

These are the kind of heterosuggestions we get from the smoking world.

All these suggestions are stored somewhere in your mind. These suggestions then become the pillars for certain beliefs in your mind. Beliefs are very powerful, and they work in our subconscious mind. This means that we don't notice that they have an influence on our daily behavior. They do, however, and in a very convincing way.

Just as an example:

It was accepted for thousands of years that no human being could run a mile in under four minutes. So, for ages and ages, nobody did. Until there was an athlete called Roger Bannister, who ran the mile in 3:59! Amazing!

What is more amazing is the fact that within the year, Bannister changed the limiting belief of the four-minute mile; several other athletes broke that so-called impossible barrier. Shows you just how powerful a belief can be. Notice that this was also a belief created by suggestions and brainwashing of society and peer groups.

Human behavior is guided by the beliefs you have. Your brain is constantly asking two questions:

When I do this, will it give me pleasure or pain?

What should I do to avoid pain and gain pleasure?

Your brain is looking for answers, and these answers are given by the beliefs you have developed through the years. These are generalizations—things you have accepted to be true. You have given a certain meaning to things and events, and these are going to determine your behavior. You could say a belief is a kind of feeling of certainty about the meaning of something; for example, that fire is hot. This is a general belief most people share.

How have you arrived at this belief? By having enough references and experiences to support it. You can compare a belief to a tabletop with legs under it. It's the legs that support the tabletop. These legs are the references and experiences you have in your life.

When we now go back to smoking, you have formed beliefs based on suggestions you get from our society, both smoking and nonsmoking society. Apart from these suggestions, what else makes you believe your belief? Is there something else that enforces the beliefs or illusions you already have?

ᘓ

5. The balloon that creates the emptiness

I magine that your body has a small balloon inside it. Let's say that we have a balloon for each addiction that exists. The balloon is just lying there. It doesn't cause any harm since it's not inflated. For the same reason, we don't feel anything because it's not inflated.

When you smoke your first cigarette, what happens? Nicotine is a very fast drug. It goes through your veins and blood and, in no time, the nicotine has found its way to the nicotine balloon, and it starts to inflate the balloon for the first time. By inflating the balloon, the balloon is pushing aside some of your intestines and fighting to claim its spot in your body. Because the balloon is inflating gradually, you are not aware of this change in your body.

From the moment you extinguish your cigarette, the balloon starts to deflate again, leaving behind an open space. Every time you light another cigarette, the balloon inflates again, and it becomes a support for your intestines. When your cigarette is finished, the balloon starts to deflate again and starts creating an empty feeling in your stomach.

This empty feeling is caused by the deflated balloon that now is no longer supporting your intestines. The balloon has created a vacuum in your body, and your body wants to fill up this vacuum again. This is a way to describe the empty feeling you feel when you haven't smoked for a while.

Your body starts creating a need for a cigarette and nicotine. Without nicotine, without the inflated balloon inside, you start feeling uncomfortable because of this vacuum, this hungry feeling you have inside. From the moment you light a cigarette, the balloon inflates and you feel comfortable again. You feel sure and supported because of the inflated balloon.

Actually, when you smoke, you feel the same as the moment before you started smoking. This is important to understand. When you smoke a cigarette, you take yourself and your body back to the condition it was in before you ever started smoking! If it's not clear or if you are still confused about this sentence, read it again and think about it for a while. Let it really sink into your mind, and make sure you fully understand what we mean here.

When you smoke a cigarette, you take yourself back to the same condition you were in before you started smoking! What are the effects of this? How do we understand this? What are the causes?

First, do you agree with what I've said above? Maybe you don't, and if so, I politely ask you to reread what is written.

Most smokers believe they gain something when they smoke. They believe that by smoking, they get something extra that nonsmokers don't have. As a smoker, you have the feeling of certainty when you smoke, a feeling of power in a difficult situation, a friend in a difficult moment, a relief when stressed—all feelings we believe that we have and nonsmokers don't have.

I can still vividly remember making a trip through the United States of America with my parents. I was twenty-one that summer, and in those days it was a big deal for a family from Belgium to go on vacation to the United States. The whole family was looking forward to it; I would finally visit my dream country! We were going to the areas I wanted to see the most. We were going to go to the West Coast. California, Arizona, Nevada, the Grand Canyon, Yellowstone Park, and *Marlboro Country*—Monument Valley.

My room at home was already filled with every possible poster about *Marlboro Country*, so I could imagine how the countryside looked. When I looked at the pictures of the cowboys and the horses, I could feel the breeze and hear the sound of the birds in the sky.

Then I was actually standing in Monument Valley! So I lit a cigarette with my Zippo and took a deep pull. What a feeling. I felt I was in control of the whole world. I was calm, relaxed, and enjoying the wonderful view over Monument Valley. And I was thankful that I could share this moment with a cigarette in my mouth. Without this cigarette, the experience wouldn't have been as nice; at least that's what I thought then and there.

It's the balloon feeling that gives us this impression. When the balloon is inflated, we feel great. When the balloon is empty, we feel like we are missing something; we feel hungry, and we feel the same as when we are in love. We have butterflies in our stomach. Remember this feeling for later on, because we will come back to this when we speak about withdrawal pains.

So when the balloon is inflated, we believe that we feel better than a nonsmoker does. Well, my parents were also admiring the view and the nature at Monument Valley, and they felt at least as great as I did. They weren't smoking! I could see my sister was enjoying the view, and she wasn't smoking. At that time I didn't think about this; it took a lot of reflection and thinking before I finally realized how I, as the smoker, was fooling myself.

I started to realize that I was actually smoking to gain back the feelings and condition I had before I started smoking. Once you become a nicotine addict and you start smoking a pack a day, the balloon soon gets worn out. This means that no matter how much you smoke, you are never able to regain exactly the same level of comfort as when you were a nonsmoker.

So no matter what you smoke or when you smoke, you'll always be left with a slightly uncomfortable feeling. Those butterflies never go away completely. This is one of the reasons that eat at the self-esteem of a smoker.

You'll get the feeling that you're constantly missing something, no matter how much you smoke. The moment you stop smoking, this feeling becomes bigger, and therefore you'll light a cigarette even more quickly than before.

As we have seen earlier, this is what we imagine! The reality is that there was nothing missing before we started to smoke. The missing feeling, the hungry feeling, the butterflies, the balloon effect are all created by smoking that first cigarette! Before you smoked that first cigarette, you were missing nothing. We didn't have this hungry feeling or anything like it. So this balloon effect describes how the nicotine is working in our body. In addition, it does this very, very slowly, so that we are not aware of the fact that we have become addicted to it.

Society, with all its contradictory information, makes us curious. Then there is the awful taste that creates our first strong belief about smoking. You never believe you'll get hooked on such an awful product. Then there is the balloon effect of the nicotine that slowly grows in our body, creating the vacuum that will give us that hungry, missing feeling.

Another aspect of nicotine is that it works the other way around. It's only when we don't smoke that we will feel the balloon effect or the butterflies. So the nicotine causes us to brainwash ourselves by saying that we feel bad or less comfortable when we don't smoke. We believe that when we smoke, we have something extra over nonsmokers.

When you are in a relaxed environment, after a good movie, after a nice meal, while meeting with friends, and you light up a cigarette, what happens? You feel more relaxed. You feel more comfortable. Why? Because you blew up the balloon, and by doing this you remove the hungry feeling; you remove the vacuum that was in your body.

A minute before you light the cigarette, even while you are feeling great and relaxed after that movie or meal, there is this insecure and hungry feeling in you. After you light the cigarette, the balloon effect disappears and you don't feel that hungry feeling anymore, and so you feel much better. Therefore, you think that the nonsmoker was feeling as you felt a minute ago, and now you are feeling better, so the nonsmoker is missing something.

However, the opposite is true. The nonsmoker already felt like this from the very beginning. You are just trying to catch up. However, because it works the opposite way around, you don't jump to this conclusion.

Imagine you start missing something; you start to get the hungry feeling, from the moment you light up the cigarette. Would you continue smoking? Would you understand the cause of this feeling of deprivation? I believe you would. And you would be able to come to the right conclusion. Now it's the opposite. By lighting the cigarette, you set the causes in motion. However, you'll only start feeling the effects when you extinguish the cigarette.

In addition to brainwashing, nicotine creates other effects in your mind. Think for a second: when are some of the occasions you really need a cigarette? In difficult moments, you grab a cigarette to help you, to assist you. Therefore, the cigarette becomes your partner—in some cases, maybe your best friend who is always there for you whenever you light him up!

Therefore, the thoughts about nicotine and cigarettes become positive ones. Every time you are in a difficult situation, the cigarette comes to help you out. The actual truth is the opposite. Let's assume you are in a stressful or difficult situation. You haven't smoked for a while, so you start feeling deprived of something, and you feel the balloon effect taking place in your body and feel even worse.

When you light up a cigarette, you start feeling better because you removed the balloon effect. You conclude that you feel less miserable than before and that the cigarette helped you to accomplish this. Actually, you feel exactly the same, and you just paused for a short time while the balloon effect took place.

The damage is done. Your brain believes that the cigarette helps to relieve stress and better overcome difficult situations. This will play an important role in the quitting process. You'll think about your cigarettes as a good partner and a friend. The belief we implant in our brain is that a cigarette provides us with pleasure and in difficult situations is a friend who relieves our pressure.

The question of how many cigarettes you need is also answered by the balloon effect that takes place in your body. As we saw, the balloon effect creates a vacuum in your body. This means that from the moment you light a cigarette, the balloon is inflated almost like an airbag in a car. The difference with an airbag is the deflation process. Once inflated, the balloon in our body will deflate very slowly; we almost don't feel it.

Therefore, the missing feeling or hungry feeling does not come at once; it comes very, very slowly. After about an hour, the balloon is completely deflated, and thus the vacuum feeling, the hungry feeling, has reached its highest point. We can hold out until then because the balloon feeling was progressing so slowly that we hardly felt it. Now the balloon is completely empty and we can feel the vacuum.

That's why we light another cigarette. We inflate the balloon again, we remove the uncomfortable feeling and we can stand the increasing balloon effect for the next hour. Once you start smoking more and more, you decrease the deflation time, which means that the balloon will become empty more quickly. Therefore, the hungry, uncomfortable way you feel will increase.

This then makes you light up another cigarette. Quite simple, isn't it. This is another clever move by the nicotine addiction. It gets worse and worse while the smoker believes he gets it better and better under control. The fact is, he removes the hungry feeling more quickly. The fact remains that he is causing the balloon effect to happen more quickly. This balloon effect, this hungry feeling, is the same as for any other addiction.

Before you were addicted, there was no emptiness; then you started smoking or drinking or using another drug, and you inflated the balloon in your body. From that moment on, you are addicted. You have created the vacuum, and you'll try to return to the state you were in before you started with your addiction.

Have you ever wondered why you don't like to go to the theater anymore? Have you been at a reception and gotten nervous with the people around you, for no good reason? Have you had the feeling in a meeting that you absolutely wanted to get out?

If you have had these feelings, and I'm quite sure you have had them, it's for one reason. You had to have a cigarette! I can remember how I hated our family reunions, simply because of the fact that I couldn't smoke at the table, and we sat at the table for five or six hours.

We Belgians love all the goodies from the kitchen, and parties can go on for hours! No matter which dish would come to the table, I was already less hungry because I was thinking when I could escape from the table to have a smoke. In the beginning I tried telling everybody I had to go to the bathroom, but I couldn't tell people I had to go ten or fifteen times during one dinner!

It was the same with long meetings at work. My concentration would drop rather quickly. After a while, I focused on when I could smoke my next cigarette! Pathetic, isn't it? I now believe that I missed some good opportunities because of this. It became even worse when I became a management consultant. I traveled all over the world helping companies improve their businesses, and, depending on which country I was working in, the company policies towards smoking were different. In the United States, at least in the companies I visited, it was simple: no smoking inside the building. In Europe it changed from country to country, Western Europe following the trend of the United States, central Europe still behind on the smoking issue.

Depending on the smoking conditions of the company, my quality of work suffered. When I couldn't smoke in the office, I had to go outside every five to ten minutes to have a cigarette. This created a bad image with the client, which I then had to go and explain. When I think back to it, it's really sad how I let cigarettes ruin so many great moments.

Once, on a sunny September day, I was having dinner with a colleague. We were in a small town by the ocean outside Boston. We were sitting on a nice terrace with a wonderful view over the ocean. The moment I sat down, I lit a cigarette while my colleague ordered a nice aperitif. When the waitress came out with the aperitifs, she kindly reminded me that they didn't allow smoking in their restaurant. I remarked that I was aware of that and that was the reason why we decided to sit outside.

She said, however, smoking wasn't allowed on the terrace. That made my blood boil, and I asked why smoking was forbidden on the terrace and who would possibly be bothered by it. She said that it was not about disturbing anybody or any other reason. It was the law, and nothing more.

I became furious!

I asked if smoking anywhere outside was forbidden or if it was just limited to that restaurant. She said that outside was fine as long as it was not on the premises of the restaurant. So I took the table and placed it in such a way that my chair was outside the boundaries of the restaurant while my colleague was still sitting within the property of the restaurant. That was my solution. I don't need to tell you that I didn't really enjoy the dinner and the nice view of the ocean.

It's amazing what the balloon effect makes us do. It's the power, that enormous power of nicotine, which is, in fact, a very potent drug. Although the balloon effect is real and we do feel those butterflies and empty feeling, it doesn't really hurt. All smokers are afraid of quitting because of the withdrawal pains that go along with it.

Well, let me tell you something that might comfort you. You have already experienced the withdrawal pains a thousand times or more! Yes, you heard me right: as a smoker, you actually go through withdrawal pains on a daily basis. That's mainly the reason why you light a new cigarette.

You light up only because you feel those butterflies; you feel the vacuum.

Does it hurt? Is it painful? No, it's not. I agree it's a kind of strange, hungry feeling. But would you ever go to see a doctor and tell him you are suffering from a hungry feeling that hurts so much that you can't stand it anymore? Of course not. Every smoker survives this feeling many times a day. The longer you wait before smoking another cigarette, the stronger the balloon effect or hungry feeling gets.

But you won't die from it, right? So why should quitting smoking remain so difficult? What effect does the balloon have on us if it's not withdrawal pains? What would we miss by quitting? I can imagine some of your heartbeats now. You hear the word "quitting" and a panic feeling becomes the master of your body. I understand; I went through it as well. As long as you smoke, just the thought of quitting can give you a real panic attack.

Why?

Where is this feeling coming from? What do we think we will miss when we stop smoking? We have already seen that we can't actually miss anything, because we created the balloon by starting to smoke and now we just try to go back to our original situation before we smoked, so what are we afraid of?

First of all, as we have already seen, the balloon effect causes us to have the hungry feeling. Second, our brain now believes that cigarettes help us when we feel bored or need to concentrate. Although this is contradictory, we believe it. We all think that the cigarette is our partner, our best friend, in difficult situations.

So when you think about quitting, naturally you get a bit stressed, and you believe that this will be a difficult situation. And who do you normally need in such circumstances? Right, your pal, Mr. Cigarette!

But you can't have Mr. Cigarette anymore. That's why you are panicking. That's also the reason why most smokers don't attempt to quit. The fear is too big to even consider it. Recall what we said earlier about fear.

~

6. Beliefs about smoking

Let's have a look at the different beliefs you have about smoking and everything associated with it. The reason we are reviewing these beliefs is quite simple. If you want to change a behavior, you have to change the beliefs that go along with this behavior. You have seen how we have been brainwashed by society, both the smoking part and the nonsmoking part.

Which beliefs has this brainwashing created in your mind?

As we will see in the next chapter, it first created a belief that actually got us hooked on smoking. In this chapter, we will focus on the beliefs we have developed as smokers. These are the beliefs that make it difficult for us to quit.

As a smoker, you believe:

- that smoking is a bad habit, not a drug addiction, and it's very difficult to break habits
- that you smoke because you choose to
- that the only way you can quit is by having a lot of willpower
- that you need a cigarette to relax or concentrate
- that your food won't taste as good anymore if you don't have a cigarette afterwards
- that you get real pleasure from smoking a cigarette
- that quitting is very difficult and almost impossible

- that you have to go through a lot of misery and pain before you finally free yourself from cigarettes
- that you'll never succeed in quitting because you are completely hooked on smoking
- that you'll never be completely free from your addiction, like other drug addicts are never really free
- that your life won't be the same without your friend, the cigarette, and that you'll miss something in your life
- that you'll have to make an enormous sacrifice to quit
- that you'll miss something very badly because you know so many people who have failed
- that you'll suffer physically by quitting because of the withdrawal pains
- that you enjoy smoking
- that you'll put on weight when you stop smoking.

Maybe you are thinking that you don't have all these beliefs, maybe just a few of them. Good, even better. The fewer beliefs you have from this list, the better. Once you are able to change these beliefs or resolve them, you are ready to smoke your last cigarette; you are ready for your big Final Liberation and megacelebration of being a free nonsmoker!

As long as you have these beliefs, you'll continue smoking, and you'll find it very difficult to quit. Even if you quit, you are bound to start again, for the simple reason that the belief is still there. Now, who is going to remove these beliefs? No, I won't do this for you. You'll do this. I'll just help you through the process.

You have already started to undermine these beliefs the moment you began reading this book. The whole purpose of this book is to help you undermine these beliefs. If you and I succeed in this endeavor, we will have a reason to celebrate, because you'll be a free person and you'll be able to stop smoking in a split second, whenever you want to.

Without any suffering.

That is why it's so important that you read this book with an open mind and in a relaxed atmosphere, even while smoking; after all, you are still a smoker. If I asked you to stop smoking before you read this book, you would be stressed, not able to concentrate, and not willing to accept any new ideas or information. Now you can enjoy as many cigarettes as you wish. As you read these pages, the information is penetrating into your mind and starting the process of your Final Liberation. Let's have a look at some of the beliefs in more detail.

Smoking is a bad habit.

We already discussed the belief about habit or drug addiction in chapter two. I believe that you have already shattered this belief. If not, I urge you to go back to chapter two, reread it carefully, and think about it for as long as you need for you to acknowledge the process and accept the fact that you have a drug addiction!

I smoke because I choose to smoke.

If, after reading the paragraphs below, you believe that you smoke because you chose to become a smoker, then we have a very big problem. Do you have children? Can you imagine yourself encouraging your children to start smoking? Can you? If the answer is no, I guess that answers this belief, doesn't it? Let us make it even clearer. If there is one reason why you or anybody else smokes, it's because you became hooked on nicotine. That's it. Even young people don't choose to smoke to be cool or great; they smoke because they become addicted to nicotine.

With everything we now know about smoking, do you really believe that anybody, including you, could be so stupid to choose this terrible poisoning for themselves? Do you believe you would make the choice to wake up every morning coughing like hell and feeling short of breath, having to look for your cigarettes every moment of the day, feeling looked down on by people, being excluded from social events, feeling that your body and condition are gradually deteriorating, having black clouds in your mind, worrying about every pain you feel in your chest or head, smelling like a pig to nonsmokers, spending a fortune on your daily poison?

Are you so stupid that you have actually chosen this? I doubt it. No, the reason is that you have become addicted to nicotine. In the next chapter we will describe how quickly it happens; nicotine is one of the fastest acting drugs that exists.

When people told me how bad my cough was and that smoking was bad for my health, I always replied that I was strong and wouldn't suffer from its bad consequences. I was a very passionate advocate to smoke and tended to get into long debates whenever the issue of the right of smoking in public places came up. I was so adamant that no real discussion was possible with me at that time. I was a smoker, a very conscious smoker, and I claimed that I was smoking only to prove to others how wrong their opinions were. Silly, isn't it?

So the good news is that you don't choose to start smoking, like the alcoholic never chooses to become an alcoholic. The one thing you might say is that, as a smoker, despite knowing all these terrible things about it, you actually choose to continue smoking. As we've already seen, this is part of nicotine addiction. But we'll come back to it later, once you understand that you have no reason to smoke because it gives you nothing.

You'll understand that you continue smoking due to the balloon effect explained in the previous chapter.

It takes a lot of willpower to quit.

Another strong belief is the belief that it takes a lot of willpower to quit. You believe it because of what you hear around you. You hear it from people who have quit, you hear it from doctors, you hear it from the cancer foundations that are helping smokers through the most difficult moments of their lives, and you hear it from all the companies that produce nicotine patches and pills: It takes a lot of willpower and discipline to quit. It's a very strong belief you have, and it can be even stronger if you have already tried to quit but failed. Then you are absolutely convinced that it takes a lot of willpower.

Let me ask you, why is it so difficult to quit? Nobody forces you to smoke. So if you decide to quit, that's it. It's over. Is this so difficult? I wish it was this easy. Then you wouldn't need to read this book. The main thing is that when somebody wants to stop smoking, he associates quitting with missing something. But if you analyze it more closely, what is the difference between you and a nonsmoker? The nonsmoker does not want a cigarette; he has no desire for a cigarette.

I remember how afraid I was when I thought about quitting. I felt embarrassed about myself. I was ashamed of my own personality. I was convinced that I didn't have any willpower; I didn't have any character because I was a smoker. These were thoughts I never spoke aloud. They just crossed my mind from time to time. Usually when I least expected them. I didn't think about quitting all the time, although thoughts about it were always at the back of my mind. Every time I had a chest pain, these underlying thoughts would come up.

The problem with these thoughts was not only that I continued to smoke, but that I was also scared to undertake any other action or adventure. I didn't have any willpower, so no matter what I did, I would fail because I lacked the character and discipline to succeed. Fortunately, I got rid of these feelings, and now I have 100 percent confidence in my actions, my character, my discipline, and myself. I also learned that it had nothing to do with willpower; it's only a matter of desire. And that's exactly what you are going to discover.

What you are going to accomplish throughout this book is similar to the thoughts of the nonsmoker. You'll remove the desire to smoke. We will guide you and help you achieve it. Once you have reached this point, you'll see that it does not take any willpower to smoke your last cigarette; on the contrary, you'll enjoy quitting, being free at last. There will be no difficulty at all because there won't be any desire to smoke left. Does this sound great? You bet! It's fantastic, and you are about to experience it. You'll free yourself from one of the biggest illusions you've had for most of your life!

I need a cigarette to relax, to concentrate, out of boredom.

You should understand the balloon effect of a cigarette by now, and you won't find it too hard to understand that this belief is also an illusion we have to get rid of. Have you ever wondered how it is that a cigarette can help you in two opposite situations—when you are completely stressed and then when you are totally relaxed? How in the world can the same product, a cigarette, help you in both situations? Doesn't it sound a bit strange to you?

As we already saw in the chapter on the balloon effect, the moment you smoked your first cigarette, the nicotine created this balloon in your body. When you extinguish a cigarette, the balloon deflates and you get that empty, hungry feeling. It's like when a mosquito bites you; you get this itching feeling, and you have a tendency to scratch it all the time.

When you are in a stressed situation, you'll have the same hungry, itchy feeling. If you now light a cigarette, this hungry feeling will disappear and you'll think and believe that you are less stressed. This happens because you are temporarily saved from this hungry, empty feeling. The reality is that you actually become even more stressed by lighting the cigarette. Due to the nicotine, your heart starts beating faster, your lungs are filled with poison and your natural defense mechanisms are set in motion. This causes your body to be more alert and stressed than before you smoked the cigarette.

I could smoke one cigarette after another when I was in a stressed situation. I often didn't even finish the first cigarette before lighting a new one. I had the impression that it was helping me, but in fact I remained stressed until the actual cause of the stress disappeared. You could tell by the number of cigarettes on the floor how long the situation lasted and how stressed I was.

Now I understand why I did it and why I had the illusion that the cigarette was actually helping me to relax. For you, a smoker, your best friend—yes, your very best friend—is your cigarette! In a stressful situation or when you need some support or help, you want to count on your best friend, the cigarette. So the more support you get, the more you call for your buddy, Mr. Cigarette. The situation is exactly the same when you feel bored and you have the illusion that the cigarette helps you to fight your boredom. You feel bored for many different reasons, so you appeal to your best friend. It's always near; you just take it out of your pocket or purse. You light the cigarette and what happens? The hungry, empty feeling disappears. The itching disappears and you feel a lot better than a few minutes ago, so you then create the illusion that you are less bored.

Without a cigarette, my food won't taste as good anymore.

This belief is one of the stronger beliefs that a smoker has. A cigarette after lunch or dinner is, for many smokers, almost a sacred ritual. What is it to you? I remember how I couldn't even wait until after dinner to smoke cigarettes. Because I was smoking so much, there were only a few occasions left when a cigarette would still taste really good to me; at least that was the illusion I had.

For many people, the cigarette after dinner is one of the best cigarettes of the day. Why? Let's have a closer look at this illusion and see if you can relate to it. Depending on the person you have dinner with, it's usually a pleasant experience. We select the food and drinks we like, we choose the company we want, we choose a place that we like and where we feel relaxed. In short, you create an atmosphere where you are fully relaxed and enjoy the moment. For a nonsmoker, this situation alone will be enough so they feel relaxed and satisfied, at least if your food tastes the way it's supposed to.

For smokers, the situation isn't ideal. Although they seem to have everything they want—nice food, the right wine with it, the right company, a nice location—there is still one thing missing. They have to fill up the balloon. No matter what or how much they eat, they still have a hungry feeling in their stomach. For them the situation is not perfect, not yet. So when, after the meal, they finally light a cigarette, everything feels wonderful again. They now feel fully relaxed without any worries, and everything is heavenly.

The smoker says, "Oh, this tastes so great, I wouldn't want to miss this." What the smokers don't realize is that the nonsmokers at the table have been enjoying these moments for a long time, and they didn't need a cigarette to do so. The smokers first had to remove the empty balloon effect before they could feel fully relaxed.

Another common fact is that smokers don't enjoy their meals and therefore try to avoid them. They try to avoid situations when they can't smoke at the table. They constantly have this hungry feeling, and because of the nonsmoking company, they can't satisfy it. Therefore, they don't enjoy the dinner; they enjoy neither the food nor the company.

Every year we had some great family parties. There were usually organized by one of the family members at his or her home or in a restaurant. No matter what the location was, I couldn't smoke at the table. Only my grandmother and my godfather smoked in our family; my father stop smoking when he was in his early thirties. As I was a part of the younger generation, it was not appropriate for me to smoke at the table. My sister always sat next to me, and she became furious whenever somebody smoked in her presence.

The only solution for me was to leave the table and go outside or to another room to have my cigarette. During a long Christmas dinner, I would leave the table six to eight times. I went outside or on the terrace to smoke my cigarette. Sometimes it was raining outside or it was very, very cold. All these things were of no importance as long as I could smoke my cigarette. In most cases, I ended up with a bad cold afterwards. The moment you become free from cigarettes, one of the great things you'll experience is how much better your food tastes! It is really amazing! You discover tastes that you forgotten existed. You'll be able to smell again. Your senses will become much stronger, and therefore you'll enjoy your drinks and dinners so much more. And you'll experience all that in just a couple of hours; you don't have to wait for this great effect to kick in weeks later. You'll truly enjoy your dinners again!

Smoking gives me a pleasure that nonsmokers don't have.

If you think back to the balloon effect a cigarette causes in your body, you understand that smoking itself does not cause pleasure. It's simply filling up the vacuum, the emptiness created by the balloon, and therefore it gives you the illusion that you enjoy it. The reality is that when you smoke, you only try to go back to the same condition you were in as a nonsmoker.

This is an important point, and I hope that you fully understand it. Understanding alone is not enough; once you understand it, you have to analyze it and then accept it. The amazing thing is that even nonsmokers believe that there has to be some pleasure in smoking. They have created this belief through the many examples provided by friends, relatives, and TV and movie stars. The references, provided by heterosuggestions, created their beliefs. Some of the nonsmokers somehow regret being nonsmokers, but since they don't miss anything, they keep on using their brains. Analyze for yourself what pleasure you really think you have from a cigarette, and the answer will finally come to you.

I would like to talk to you about the best cigarette of the day. For some of you, the best cigarette of the day is the first one you smoke. Or it could be the one you smoke after breakfast, after lunch, after sex, when driving your car, etc. No matter which one you believe is the best cigarette, answer the following questions:

How is it possible that a large group of people, smoking the same brand of cigarettes, have such different ideas about which cigarette tastes the best?

How is it possible that one cigarette, out of a pack of twenty, tastes so much better than all the other cigarettes in that pack? Are they all the same or are they different?

Do you start seeing the illusion? All twenty cigarettes in a pack are exactly the same. They all taste the same. How do they taste? They all taste exactly the same as your very first cigarette! There is absolutely no difference.

Why do you have this idea? How do you create this illusion? The answer lies again in the balloon effect of nicotine. The longer the time between your extinguishing your last cigarette and the moment you light a new one, the bigger the satisfaction with filling up the empty balloon, eliminating the vacuum and the hungry feeling. That is why many smokers find the first cigarette in the morning the best one of the day.

After a while, I smoked so much that I didn't enjoy cigarettes anymore. When I woke up during the night, I could light a cigarette, smoke it still half asleep, and go back to bed. When I woke up in the morning, I would smoke two or three cigarettes before even getting out of bed while watching television. Once out of bed, my morning coughing concert would start and last for about ten minutes. Then, time for a new cigarette. Shower, cigarette, shaving, cigarette, getting dressed, cigarette. By the time I went down to breakfast, I would have smoked six to seven cigarettes! I don't know which one was the best.

There was one cigarette I still remember as special; it was my philosophical cigarette. That cigarette actually began when I couldn't smoke inside my parents' house. I could only smoke inside my room, holding the cigarette out of the window to reduce the amount of smoke inside. Therefore, whenever I was at my parents, I smoked on the terrace, in the garden, or in my room with the window wide open. The philosophical cigarettes were those cigarettes which I smoked when it was completely dark and when everybody was already in bed. There was just me, my cigarette, and the sky with the stars and the moon. Today I enjoy such moments even more since there are no longer dark clouds overshadowing my thoughts as I admire the stars at night.

It's very difficult to quit; in fact it's practically impossible.

We discussed this belief when we spoke about willpower; nevertheless, I think it's a good idea to go into the subject a little deeper. When you believe it's very difficult to quit, it's only because you are told so! It's society and the brainwashing media that tell us how difficult it is to quit. Both sides of society give us this difficult heterosuggestion, the smokers as well as the nonsmokers.

You hear it from a friend who stops smoking for months only to go back to it. You think it must be tough, if even he couldn't make it work. You hear of hundreds and hundreds of cases: people give up smoking and then start again after a couple of months or years. You hear stories of how they suffered during those nicotine-free periods and how they missed their cigarettes. You immediately think that this won't work for you. The very thought of missing your cigarette gives you a panic attack.

Two friends of mine made a bet. They would both stop smoking, and the one who started again would pay the other $2,500!! Quite a big bet, isn't it? If both started again, they would donate their money to a cancer foundation or a hospital. The bet was already an indication of failure. If both parties were 100 percent sure of each other's success, there wouldn't be a bet. They were convinced that at least one of them would fail.

Everything went fine for the first two days. They both told me how they missed their cigarettes and that it was a tough habit to break, but they were surviving. Quite strong statements, aren't they? After four days, one of my friends started to give in. He couldn't take it anymore. He couldn't eat anymore, he couldn't sleep anymore, and he couldn't concentrate anymore. He actually said to me, "I'm no longer a human being if I can't smoke." As a smoker, you can imagine what went through my mind—the message, loud and clear, was: don't even think about quitting!

On the fifth day, we came back from a golf competition where we both played. Since I didn't play in his leg, I had no idea what happened on the course during the day. Apparently, he had been throwing his clubs and eventually lost a club in a big lake. He lost several balls, a lot more than he would normally. He made a mess of his game.

We were back in his apartment when suddenly he went down to the cellar. I asked his wife how he was handling the quitting. She said it was horrible. She hoped he would give in quickly so that he could be "normal" again. Ten minutes later, he wasn't back yet, so I decided to go to the cellar to see what he was doing. When I opened the door of the underground garage, I saw my friend, slamming his golf clubs on a concrete floor and, at the same time, yelling and screaming. It was an unbelievable sight.

Finally, I calmed my friend down; we collected the pieces of his golf clubs and went upstairs again. He destroyed about four golf clubs. Back in the apartment, he went to the table, took a pack of Marlboros, and lit a cigarette. He simply said, ""That's it, I give up. I didn't realize I would miss it so much. It's mainly the feeling of not being allowed to do something that bothers me."

And that was the end of the bet. He paid his part and he told everyone who wanted to listen about his failure. Deep in his heart, he was not proud of himself; he knew he had lost something important. He knew he was not able to regain control of his life. It was a worry for him. The excuse to the outside world was that nobody should tell him what he could or couldn't do. This was a feeling he couldn't stand. What happened to the other friend? He is a free, happy nonsmoker, and he is not missing anything; on the contrary, he understands better than most people that this bet was a one-way ticket to freedom.

Examples like this are the worst kind of brainwashing that smokers can experience. It happens all the time in your close social circle; you are involved in the process and you witness the failure of someone you trust. Why would you doubt him or her? The fact that in this case there is also a winner makes the brainwashing even stronger; you have tremendous respect for the person who quit because you know how difficult it must have been not to give up.

Throughout this book, you'll learn that it's not difficult to quit. You'll actually realize that it's one of the easiest things you have ever done in your entire life. This book will be a guide to help you come to this new belief. Quitting smoking is a very easy thing to do and it does not make you suffer for a second! The moment you smoke your last cigarette, you are already free; you immediately feel like a nonsmoker, asking yourself how in the world you could have ever started to smoke.

Isn't that amazing? Isn't that something you would absolutely like to achieve? Just read on and let your brain take care of the rest. You are almost there. Your Final Liberation is closer than you may think.

I'll have to go through a lot of misery and pain before freeing myself from cigarettes.

This belief is similar to the previous one except for one major difference; in this case, the outcome is positive. Again, the fact that you believe it's so difficult to quit is due to brainwashing done by our society. Doctors give advice on how to handle withdrawal symptoms, smokers tell great stories of how they handled their nerves in the first weeks of quitting, and there is television advertising for patches and gums. All these things make you believe that it must be very hard.

Otherwise, why would they invent all these supporting tools? Why would smokers tell their stories?

It all comes back to the initial point we discussed earlier. Why do you smoke? What is the difference between a smoker and a nonsmoker? It's really simple. A nonsmoker doesn't want a cigarette. He has absolutely no desire for a cigarette.

If you stop smoking tomorrow and you still have that desire to smoke, then you'll fail. Well, a very small percentage holds on. I really don't envy these people. They experience a really hard time. But if you don't crave cigarettes anymore, why would you still smoke? If you don't want cigarettes anymore, would it still be difficult to put them aside? No, of course not. Well, you are in the process of eliminating the need to smoke again. You are, through this book, going to remove your desire to smoke. Once you understand that all the beliefs you have about smoking, and the reason why you think you smoke, are nothing else but illusions, and that there is nothing like withdrawal symptoms, you'll be *free!* You'll never ever want a cigarette again.

I'll never be able to quit because I'm completely hooked.

Another illusion many smokers have is that because they are addicted to it, they are lost forever. Have you ever tried to quit? If the answer is yes, I presume you failed while reading this book, right? OK, let me tell you one thing: don't use the word "failed." Yes, you tried and it didn't work out. That's fine, at least you tried! Remember Thomas Edison? He failed more than ten thousand times before eventually succeeding. Would you call him a failure? I doubt it.

When you had this experience of trying unsuccessfully to quit, it created this new and strong belief in your brain that you are completely hooked and won't be able to quit. You feel like a loser; you feel very bad about it. You can lose your self-confidence because of it. Many people do. The longer it lasts, the worse it becomes, and you start doubting even more. It affects your personality, and you start losing control in other areas of your life. A setback in one field is enough to make you doubt your own capacities. You start feeling uncertain about whether you can handle the problem or not. To support you in this situation, you light another cigarette.

You have actually convinced yourself that it's impossible to quit. You have all the proof you need. You tried it, you witnessed many other similar cases and you believe the doctors; it becomes a nightmare. I smoked more than one hundred cigarettes a day, and I told myself that quitting would mean so much physical suffering that it would be irresponsible to do it. I came up with a "medical" excuse to continue smoking! I wondered many times what it would be like to quit. I never dared to take the chance. I was convinced that it wouldn't work. Because of this strong conviction, I never tried to quit.

You have probably realized that anybody can stop smoking in a split second. You won't suffer. Once you have discarded all the illusions about smoking, you'll become a free person.

I'll miss "my best friend"— Mr. Cigarette.

When you smoke, your cigarette is something you carry with you all day long. It's there in the morning when you wake up. You can count on it during the day whenever you want it. You have a good companion for your evening activities. And even at night, when needed, you can count on your best friend.

No matter what the situation, you can always count on a cigarette to be there with you. Because of the balloon effect, you have the impression that your "best friend" is always helping you, making the situation better or easier. I couldn't imagine living without cigarettes. Just the thought of it made me sick; I felt completely naked. I didn't even know how to walk into a room without a cigarette. What would people think of me? I was imagining how uncomfortable I would feel at receptions, parties, in bars. Standing there without a cigarette? Doing what? Impossible! I couldn't imagine myself working at my desk without a big ashtray next to me, filled with cigarettes. Working at my computer, I needed a strong puff every couple of seconds to get inspiration.

Watching television without a cigarette? The programs would be boring. My cigarettes were everywhere, and I couldn't imagine going through the day without them. As we have already seen, all these thoughts were just illusions created by the balloon effect. The cigarette isn't actually helping us in these situations, the only thing we try to do is to get back the feeling we had before we started smoking. That's it. It's just an illusion that the cigarette does anything substantial for us. The only thing it does is feed our addiction, fill up the balloon, and remove the hungry feeling we have in our stomach.

When you smoke your last cigarette, you'll know that you don't need cigarettes to feel good. You'll know that it was just an illusion. You'll feel like a nonsmoker again, and you won't suffer from this limiting belief anymore.

I'll have to make an enormous sacrifice in order to quit.

I understand your feelings about this belief. I believed it for years. But let's have a look at it from a distance. Let's see how well you can already analyze the situation. What sacrifice is there to make? If we miss something when we quit, it means it should give us something extra. A bonus!

You and I have seen some of the illusions, and I reckon that you have seen through them and understand the way they work. Where's the bonus of a cigarette? Yesterday evening I was discussing the subject with my girlfriend. When I first spoke to her about the Painless Stop Smoking Cure, she was a bit skeptical, which was all right with me. She had already tried to quit several times.

Although it seemed to work out in the beginning, she would always go back to smoking. One time she lasted a few months, another time more than a year. I asked her how she could restart smoking after staying away from it for more than a year. She explained that one day she arrived at her parents' home after an exhausting day. She was home alone and there was nothing to eat in the house. She found a pack of cigarettes and thought to herself, "Well, then, I'll smoke a nice, tasty cigarette." That was it. She inflated the balloon again, and she was back chain smoking in no time.

Today, she knows that a nice, tasty cigarette doesn't exist. She knows that all cigarettes taste exactly the same as the very first one—disgusting. She has broken the illusion; she has replaced this limiting belief with the thought of being free. She doesn't feel like a slave anymore. She values her freedom and health above anything. How did this happen? Unconsciously, she went through the Painless Stop Smoking Cure and reached the moment when she finally found her trigger to say, "It's enough, *never again!*"

She smoked her last cigarette with a sense of victory, feeling a huge sense of power—a power of being set free and letting go of those heavy chains she had carried for years and years. She became an enthusiastic runner. Every week she runs about ten miles. A couple of weeks ago she accomplished a milestone, with a good friend: she ran the half marathon in Brussels, finishing in a great time. Her new target is to complete a full marathon. She'll do it!

Let me tell you, you don't sacrifice anything when you smoke your last cigarette. There are absolutely no benefits whatsoever in smoking. There is so much to win when you quit. I believe that by now, you have already seen through some of the brainwashing maze. You have already liberated yourself from a couple of illusions. That's great! The others illusions will soon fall.

&

7. It tastes good

All the contradictions you hear attract you to cigarettes. Human beings are curious by nature and prefer to convince themselves of something by trial and error in order to create a new belief or to accept society's beliefs.

As your subconscious mind receives all this contradictory information, you become curious to test it out. There couldn't be a better way for you to find out what is true about cigarettes; are they as bad as some people say or are they really as good as others claim? And so you light the first cigarette…

And now comes the worst part of brainwashing; it tastes awful! The cigarette you have just lit tastes disgusting, it makes you cough, makes you feel dizzy. Therefore, the first belief you form about cigarettes is that you'll never get hooked on them. How could you get hooked on something that tastes so disgusting?

It would be a lot better if the first cigarette tasted good. Then your subconscious mind would become suspicious and wonder why it tasted so good. As a result, you would be on guard and recall all the warnings you have heard about cigarettes. But not now! This thing tastes horrible. It's impossible to get hooked on it.

And you try another one because you can't believe that your heroes from the big screen could be so wrong; you can't understand why your friends would do something so awful. You actually wonder whether you are doing something wrong. And you try another one. Of course, the taste of the cigarette remains the same. Every next cigarette tastes exactly the same as the first one you ever smoked—it tastes awful—you only become used to the taste after a while.

While you are testing who in your social group is right, you are actually becoming hooked on the cigarette and nicotine. You are not aware of it because you are convinced (it's your belief) that you can never get hooked on such an awful thing! You don't realize that you are hooked on nicotine because it happens gradually and it doesn't hurt; it's just a funny feeling you have in your stomach whenever you need a cigarette.

To add to your conviction, when you don't smoke for a while, then light a cigarette, you feel more relaxed and less nervous. So you finally start to understand your peer group and heroes, and you have to admit that smoking helps you to relax.

This explains how you get addicted to nicotine and why it becomes difficult to quit once you are really hooked. One thing is certain: if smoking were just a matter of taste, nobody would ever smoke more than one cigarette! Let's now have a look at the addiction itself so that you can better understand how it works and why you believe it's so difficult to quit.

ॐ

8. Why one cigarette doesn't exist

People sometimes ask whether it's possible to smoke cigarettes occasionally. With the knowledge you have at this point, I'm sure you are able to formulate an answer with me. Firstly, there is your balloon, the empty feeling in your stomach. The moment you smoke another cigarette, the balloon reappears, it inflates immediately and then begins to deflate. This creates the hungry feeling in your stomach.

Secondly, there is brainwashing by society that tells you that smoking gives you a certain pleasure, and that when you don't smoke, something is missing in your life. These are exactly the feelings you experience when you only smoke occasionally. This creates a strong feeling of suffering for you, feeding society's brainwashing that smoking has some benefits to the smoker.

Most people that get addicted are not free. When they stop smoking, they still have the feeling of missing something. They were not consciously aware of that feeling. Unconsciously, they still felt they were deprived of something. They didn't completely remove the desire to smoke. Therefore, when they find themselves in a situation when in the past they would have smoked a cigarette, they light a new one thinking they need it. This is strongly influenced by heterosuggestions from our society.

Imagine you are in a stressed situation. You know that a cigarette doesn't help you at all when you are stressed. However, you remember that in the past you used to smoke a cigarette when you were stressed. Your environment suggests that a cigarette helps you cope with stress. Remember the power of the heterosuggestions. This power is very strong. That's why you have to remove all the desire for cigarettes by applying adequate suggestions about the truth about cigarettes. In principle, you should not avoid situations or occasions. Since you have no more desire to smoke cigarettes, there is no situation in which you would get the desire to smoke.

Remember that a nonsmoker doesn't have the desire to smoke. It's a good idea to behave exactly the same as you did before. The reason for this is quite simple. If, after quitting, you stop doing things you used to do when you were smoking, you could experience feeling deprived.

If there was one situation or place to avoid, then it would probably be a smoky, nicotine-filled place, like a bar or pub. The reason I say this is not because you could get tempted by smelling the cigarette smoke. You surely won't get tempted by this. The problem is the nicotine that's in the air. As you know by now, the only reason you started smoking in the first place was because of nicotine addiction.

Nicotine is one of the fastest drugs that exist. Imagine you are a happy nonsmoker for months and you enter a very small bar crowded with people, of whom 80 percent are smokers. There is hardly any fresh air around. It may be that the portion of nicotine you inhale is enough to immediately inflate your balloon again. From then on, you start experiencing this hungry, empty feeling all over again, while the balloon gradually deflates. This feeling, combined with the constant heterosuggestions, can make you doubt again. And that would be a pity, wouldn't it?

Wouldn't it be the same for someone who has never smoked? Well, in the beginning you were exactly such a person. Remember, before you ever started smoking, you were not missing anything. Now that you are a nonsmoker again, you are not missing anything. There is no desire; you don't want to smoke, as nobody ever wanted to. Therefore, the situation is exactly the same. The nicotine is working as fast and as effectively as always. Why do you think approximately 80 percent of the people in this bar are smokers?

Once you have stop smoking using the Painless Stop Smoking Cure, you'll no longer have any desire for a cigarette. This is the main difference between the Painless Stop Smoking Cure and many other methods of quitting.

If you quit due to hypnosis or acupuncture, you don't smoke anymore, which is great! The thing is that your desire to smoke has not been removed. You'll always feel that you are making a sacrifice, that you are missing something. This, combined with the balloon effect and the heterosuggestions, will give you a hard time. You'll constantly doubt whether you did a good thing or not and wonder what you are missing.

With the Painless Stop Smoking Cure, you, and nobody else, have removed the desire for a cigarette. You have no reason to smoke. You have removed the craving for a cigarette. It's no longer a possibility, like a nonsmoker can never have the desire to smoke. Always remember that neither you nor anybody else missed anything before smoking that first cigarette!

Once you fully understand and accept this, you are open to let it sink into your mind. You won't have the desire to smoke anymore. You can smoke if you want to, but you won't, because you won't see any reason for it whatsoever. So you won't crave a cigarette anymore.

You'll continue to get heterosuggestions from your close social circle. You know at this moment that these heterosuggestions, together with the balloon effect, are the main reasons why people smoke and continue to smoke.

Once you have quit, these things will just continue. Your relatives and friends don't want to cause you any harm when they talk to you. They don't realize the dangerous effect their words can have on you. You feel completely free, happy and liberated from a heavy, deadly ballast in your life. Then you meet one of your friends, who wants to know how you have coped without cigarettes for so long. He wants to know if it is difficult, how you feel, and he is amazed you have managed to quit.

You hear the words "give up" smoking. These words imply that you, as a new nonsmoker, are missing out on something, when in fact you aren't! However, that is the perception of your friends and family. If you have friends that continue to smoke, you'll get another heterosuggestion. They will ask you if they can help you, if they can comfort you in any way. They will even offer you a cigarette when you are stressed or when they think you need something. Deep down, they are jealous that you stopped smoking, because, like all smokers, they wish they could become nonsmokers. When you reply by saying that you feel great and completely free and that you don't miss a thing, they won't like you for it. Deep down they even might be angry with you; certainly they envy you.

Does this mean you have to avoid smokers? On the contrary! While you will receive many heterosuggestions from them, you can also give them some new suggestions. When they finally acknowledge that you are a happy nonsmoker, full of energy and enjoying every minute of your life, they will get some positive images for themselves. For a change, they won't witness the failure of someone who tried to quit. They will see a victory, a liberation from this eternal slavery they are still bound to. In this way, you can help them and give them the courage for the moment when they feel ready to stop smoking.

The same principle applies to all social occasions. Don't avoid them! Yes, you might become the hot topic of the night, but there's nothing wrong with that. You should feel great that people ask questions about how you did it. You should be happy to answer their questions about smoking and how hard it is to quit.

By doing this you achieve two things.

First, you don't have the feeling that you are missing something, because you keep going to all the social occasions you used to go in the past. And second, you gain a strong and constructive feeling of contributing.

By sharing your message of joy and freedom, you make a huge contribution to society. Although you might feel you are insignificant in comparison with the huge power of heterosuggestion, your contribution will help make a difference in the end. There are the testimonials of millions before and after you. They will all bring the same message to the world: Quitting smoking is the easiest thing to do, there is absolutely nothing you'll miss, and you'll be a free person forever!

It's OK to think about smoking and cigarettes. It would be wrong *not* to think about cigarettes. Why? Just for the psychological missing effect. When you smoked like me, for more than twenty-five years, smoking becomes an important part of your life. Therefore, it would be completely wrong to forbid yourself from thinking about smoking and cigarettes. Furthermore, just the fact of telling yourself not to think about something will make you think about it, won't it?

When I stopped smoking that famous day, I remember how I would observe all the situations I used to light a cigarette in. I fully enjoyed this process, and it made my days even more wonderful. Therefore, I advise you to think about smoking and cigarettes once you have smoked your last cigarette.

I don't advise that you keep cigarettes and ashtrays in the house; throw away that filthy stuff! On the other hand, I always loved Zippos. They are metal lighter scomposed of two parts with a wick in it, fuelled by gas oil. When they use a lighter in movie, eight times out of ten, it's a Zippo. I have to admit, it's a great product and it has a lot of charm. It even offers a lifetime guarantee.

I collected Zippos when I was a smoker, and I continue to collect them now as a nonsmoker. That's fine. There is nothing wrong with it. Do you know what one of my biggest fears was when I was thinking about quitting smoking? That I would miss my Zippo in my left pocket of my jeans!! Unbelievable, isn't it? I was really afraid I would miss my

Zippo in my pocket. I even told myself that it was one of the reasons why I continued to smoke. If I smoked, I would always have my Zippo with me. I loved to play with my Zippo, and I knew all the tricks of opening and lighting it. When I think back, I find it so funny that I was afraid to miss it. I still think back to it with warm feelings, and I'll always find it the best lighter in the world, but I don't miss it.

You know why?

I have nothing to light. It's that simple. Telling myself I would miss my lighter was an illusion; it was the big nicotine suggestion at work. I thought I would miss a cigarette if I stopped smoking. Since the nicotine suggestion did not want me to see through this illusion, it created another illusion—that I would miss my Zippo instead. I have just recently bought two nice Zippos at a flea market in Barcelona. I noticed that even though it had been a long time since I used one, I could still do all the tricks!

There is nothing wrong in thinking about smoking or cigarettes. If, however, you think about it with desire, as if you miss something, then there is something wrong. This won't happen to you now because you are applying the Painless Stop Smoking Cure, which removes any feelings of desire or craving.

Once you have no desire for a cigarette anymore, once you don't want to smoke anymore, once you completely understand that there are absolutely no benefits in smoking, why would you want to smoke one more cigarette? You wouldn't! You simply don't want to do it. You have no reason for lighting a cigarette, so you don't do it.

There is no alternative. You have gotten to a point where you are absolutely certain that you don't want to smoke anymore. Based on this certainty, you have made a decision—I mean a true decision, meaning that there is no other way. So, why would you want to smoke just one more cigarette?

It's just impossible. It's not happening. Often people ask whether it would be a problem if, after quitting, they smoked a cigarette occasionally. Well, of course it would matter! You would be a drug addict again. The point is that only people who are still smokers can ask this question. And the reason they ask this question is because they haven't convinced themselves yet. They still doubt and are full of fear about whether they are going to succeed or not, whether they are going to miss something or not.

Imagine a nonsmoker asking if it's OK to smoke a cigarette once in a while? Sounds absurd, doesn't it? Well, indeed, it does. Nonsmokers have no reason to even think about smoking one cigarette because they have no desire for it. And, as educated nonsmokers, they know that there is absolutely nothing that a cigarette can give them. Nothing at all.

When you quit, you quit. Final. No more cigarettes, not even one. You'll see, as you continue reading, that you won't even think about cigarettes again. If you smoked that one cigarette, the nicotine would immediately inflate the balloon and you would need to start again from the beginning. But feel confident; it just won't happen. In case you still feel panicky when you think about quitting, consider this: how would you feel if I told you that you would never be able to stop smoking?

I mean, how would you feel if I or somebody else told you that you would not be able to quit, that you were doomed to smoke forever? How would you feel then?

℃

9. Why pills and patches don't work

When I started work this morning, I opened my homepage to check the latest news and got really mad. There was a huge web advertisement asking the following question: "Why do you need medicine to help you quit?" You have no idea how angry this nonsense made me! After I calmed down, I decided to have a look at what the ad had to say. Not that this company could surprise me with anything, but since I was working on this chapter, I thought it could be a good introduction. So let me take you to the company's website.

In the entire website, I couldn't find the answer to the question, why do you need medicine to stop smoking? That was the first amazing discovery. Well, not really amazing, since you and I already know that we absolutely *don't need* any pills or medicine!

Let us have a look at what the company wrote on the first page of its website: "It's now recognized that addiction to nicotine is the main reason why people keep smoking." Wow! They are almost right; it's *the only* reason. But since the people at the company haven't read my book yet, I can't blame them for not knowing this. "Most smokers don't continue to smoke out of free will but because they are addicted to nicotine." Good, they are improving. "Per year, only 2 percent-3 percent are able to quit."

That is a dramatic figure, isn't it?

It's by reading such nonsense that you get brainwashed and are so afraid that you won't even try quitting. "Approximately 50% of young smokers will still be smokers when they are sixty." Are they actually claiming that at least 50% of young smokers will make it to their sixties in a healthy way? I wouldn't dare to claim such a thing.

Now comes the best part of the brainwashing:

"This is important because it proves why it's so difficult to quit. You need to look for help to support your quit trial as well as possible. Your doctor, his assistant, or your pharmacist knows how difficult it is to overcome the addiction to nicotine and can review with you the different options you have. Smoking is not only a habit; it's much stronger than that. This realization helps you to look for effective ways to quit, discussed in the chapter 'The Cycle of Nicotine Addiction.'"

Let's review this. Do you see the brainwashing? "...Because it proves why it's so difficult to quit." Where is the proof? I don't see it. The only thing one can conclude on the basis of these figures is that the situation itself is bad and that people use a very inefficient way to stop smoking, if they attempt it at all. Maybe there are only 2 percent or 3 percent that want to quit.

Of course, I know this is not the case but I just want to show that these figures mean nothing and certainly don't prove that quitting would be difficult. The other sentence is even more destructive: "You need to look for help to support your quit trial as well as possible. Your doctor, his assistant, or your pharmacist knows how difficult it is to overcome the addiction to nicotine and can review with you the different options you have."

Words like "help," "support," "trial," and "as well as possible" don't give a lot of confidence when read in a message encouraging you to start doing something. For me and probably for you as well, they have the opposite effect. Our subconscious mind will definitely interpret it as a very difficult task ahead with little or no chance of success. Companies like this one continue to imprint this belief on our minds by saying that even your doctor knows how difficult it is. Woah! When your doctor knows it, it must be true, right? That's brainwashing.

You believe these strong societal references, and as a result you create the belief that quitting is very difficult and that you need assistance in the form of pills, medicine, or something else.

The web article continues by saying, "it's not only a bad habit." It's not a habit!! Period. It's a drug addiction, nothing else! Finally, the icing on the cake, you should "look for effective ways to quit." So here, at least, they admit that there are ineffective ways to quit. They forget to say that their advice is one of them. Which effective way? Those pills and patches.

This website is for a product from one of the biggest pharmaceutical giants in the world!!! Do you need more explanation on this one? These wrong suggestions make me so angry. You know why? Because of such messages, I didn't dare quit for years. I was so terribly brainwashed into believing that quitting was extremely difficult that I never even considered it. It made me a strong defender of the idea of being a conscious smoker, a point I could debate for hours.

Hundreds of thousands of people are misled by these messages, maybe even you, too, and because of these messages, they don't even consider quitting smoking because they see it as something unattainable. And that makes me very angry. All those thousands of people, or even millions, continue smoking, not because it's difficult to quit. No, they continue because there are some industry giants that recognize a huge market for their pills and patches.

They first create the "fact": the irreversible "truth" that quitting smoking is not only the most difficult thing to do but actually impossible without extra help. Even worse is the fact that some doctors, who should truly care about people's health in general, are sponsoring this industrial brainwashing. Those thousands or millions of people are unable to see one very simple and powerful truth:

"Quitting smoking is the easiest thing you can do, once you know how to do it!"

That is the only message in this book. Everybody can stop smoking, including *you!* And it's so simple! You won't suffer, and you certainly don't need any pills or medicine to help you. You may want to know if these products are bad products, especially if you know someone who quit with the help of pill X or gum Y. What I'm basically saying is that when people quit by taking these pills or patches, they quit despite the fact that they use these things.

The nicotine gum and patches are the worst products available because, even though you stop smoking, the balloon effect remains alive in your body. It's possible to obtain products that work on the psychological side of the addiction, which is an improvement and could have an important role to play in the future of quitting.

The main thing however, remains that when you decide to use a support, in whatever form, you automatically set yourself up for failure. That is the sad side of all these products. You are actually telling you that you can't quit on your own and therefore you need the help of product X or Y. The unfortunate truth is that there is only one person in the world that can fight your nicotine addiction, and that person is YOU! So when you think about the products described above, you already know that they won't work.

The Painless Stop Smoking Cure will teach you how *you* can quit. Nobody else can help you with it, only you. And you know something? It's very easy!! Let's have a look at the best way to kill the nicotine balloon. As long as you keep feeding the nicotine balloon, you won't be able to quit, and you certainly won't be able to kill the nicotine balloon.

As I promised you at the beginning of this book, helping you to quit is not my sole objective. It is more important that I help and guide you to conquering the nicotine balloon, since this is the only way to stop smoking without suffering! And that is exactly what I promised you: quitting in an easy, smooth, and painless way. As we will see in this chapter, the only way to achieve this is to stop feeding the balloon and constantly use your mind. If you are interested in quitting just for a while, you probably don't need this book. You can stop smoking and restart as many times as you want. The problem is that you'll never really have that feeling of total freedom and victory, and you'll be constantly suffering from a longing feeling. This book is meant to be your guide to achieving the total, long-lasting freedom you want and regaining control of your body and your environment, which is one of the best feelings a human being can have. Isn't that what you really want?

One of the myths you have to stop believing is that patches and nicotine gums are an easy way to stop smoking. The reality is the opposite. Nevertheless, a lot of organizations and doctors keep promoting these "sweeties" for the nicotine balloon. If I were to ask you about the possible ways of killing a huge dangerous animal without using any weapons, injections, etc., and without taking any risk of getting hurt in the process, what would your strategy be?

Would you agree that a rather natural way of killing a living being is to stop feeding it? Does this make sense, or do you think the animal will weaken and die quicker if you continue to feed it? It seems to be more reasonable to stop feeding the animal right away rather than to continue feeding it.

For all living beings, it's a fact that they must be fed in one way or another. If they don't get food, whatever that food might be, they will lose energy, they won't be able to maintain their vital functions, and, finally, they will cease to exist—they will die. The same applies to the nicotine balloon. It's a living thing. It's fully alive in your body and even more in your mind! I must make this clear to you; it's alive and living inside your body and mind. Understanding and accepting this is a very important step towards the elimination of the balloon.

If you don't believe that it's alive and is living inside of you, it will be very difficult to defeat it. It would be like fighting against an enemy you don't even believe exists. Once you accept the existence of the nicotine balloon, you can take the next step, the step of elimination. Through what we have covered in previous chapters, and by developing your thinking process, you should be in a position where you clearly and fully understand the existence of the nicotine balloon inside your body and mind.

Mental defeat is the biggest problem with patches and gums. You suffer from an addiction, and by using these patches, you admit that you can't beat your addiction on your own. You need extra help to overcome your addiction. You accept the power of the nicotine balloon, and at the same time you tell yourself that you are going to lose the battle.

It's the same as a stuntman who tells his crew to come and visit him in the hospital or tells them what songs to play at his funeral. You won't find a lot of these stuntmen alive, since those who follow such reasoning are probably already dead. The living stuntmen know how important a positive mental attitude is in order to succeed.

There is nothing different in conquering the nicotine balloon. You will need a positive mental attitude and total conviction about your victory, even before you make your first attempt. This is very important. If you try to fight the balloon without being fully prepared and convinced about your victory, you'll lose the battle and therefore create the same mental process as the patches do. You'll suffer from mental defeat, and you won't have another try.

By using patches and gums, you not only admit mental defeat but also keep feeding the balloon! As we have seen before, the nicotine balloon has quite specific properties; the less you feed it, the stronger and more difficult it becomes to defeat.

The patches and gums make it more difficult to quit than when you try to do it without them. Those patches with nicotine make it difficult to quit because the balloon is still doing its part of the brainwashing. It still gives you the impression that you miss something and you still get this hungry, empty feeling from time to time.

You may hear that quitting is terrible and, thanks to a patch, it became tolerable. Actually, the opposite is true. After a couple of weeks or months, you'll find most of these people have a cigarette between their lips. Once more, the nicotine wins while you end up with another example of how difficult it is to quit and make it work in the long run.

You may wonder why doctors are part of this brainwashing. Frankly, I don't know. I guess it's mostly out of ignorance. I don't blame them for this. Nobody is perfect. I would be the last person to claim that I know something about the medical side of smoking. I only know what I discovered for myself. This was a huge revelation for me. I know that it works. I know that it's easy and that everybody can apply it.

The main difference with my method and all the other methods, patches, pills, and medicines is that I don't force you to do anything you don't want to do. You do whatever you think and feel is best. You take away the desire to smoke. You are the person saying, "I don't want to smoke anymore. I don't need this cigarette anymore. I don't need nicotine to feel good. I'm free, and I'm a liberated person that can truly enjoy my freedom and life. Moreover, I am thankful to myself for taking this final easy step." Let's move onto the next chapter and look at who is controlling your daily life.

⤬

10. What will happen to your weight?

What's the effect of cigarettes and nicotine on our weight? Well, I am neither a doctor nor a body weight specialist, so I can only give you my humble opinion based on my experience. At the same time, I certainly don't want to, as so many other books and tapes about quitting smoking do, sell you hot air.

It's better to ask what the effect is of no cigarettes on your weight, because that is what many people are actually interested in. That is another illusion that makes so many people continue smoking. They have a belief that smoking keeps their weight down. Women, especially, continue to smoke because they are afraid that after quitting, they will gain weight.

This is a very good example of the pain-pleasure principle. Women associate massive pain with gaining weight, compared with getting cancer in thirty years or so. Because they link so much pain with putting on weight, they don't even consider quitting smoking.

When they eventually quit and consequently gain some weight, they associate so much pain with this situation that they start smoking again. This way they free themselves from the massive pain they feel now, the pain of putting on some weight. Let us go back briefly to the balloon effect created by the nicotine in our body. As a smoker, you have probably experienced this hungry, empty feeling in your stomach on a daily basis. This feeling is always there, and it's the result of the deflating nicotine balloon. The more it gets deflated, the bigger the hungry, empty feeling.

Once you become a regular smoker, your hungry feeling is biggest in the morning. That is why the first thing most smokers do in the morning is smoke a cigarette. By doing so, they remove the hungry feeling so that they can start the day. One of the side effects of that behavior is the lack of proper breakfast habits.

When I think back to my breakfast as a smoker, I still find it hard to believe that I could go on like that. As you remember from a previous chapter, I would smoke between five and seven cigarettes before getting to the breakfast table. Then, a few glasses of Coca-Cola and that was it. That was my typical breakfast.

Even without being a doctor or dietician, I do know that skipping breakfast is a fast lane to becoming overweight. You deny your body the energy it needs for the day. Besides that, you are running around with two hungry feelings now, one because of your nicotine balloon and the other because you are actually very hungry. So what will probably happen is that you'll snack a little bit here, a little bit there. Your body, remembering that it received no energy this morning, will save all the extra energy for the next time it's denied its daily needs. All this saved energy is then transformed into fat and sugars that remain in your body. And then you gain weight.

The idea that as a smoker you eat less is not true' it's just another illusion. As a smoker, you have this hungry, balloon feeling. Once you become a regular smoker, you'll always have the feeling of being hungry.

As you remember, the only withdrawal symptom that exists is the hungry feeling. Because you feel hungry, you eat more; you snack more on things all day long. At the end of the day, you will still have this hungry feeling, since it's always there to some extent. Unconsciously you tell yourself that you must have eaten very little since you still have this hungry feeling. The truth is that you have been eating more because you are a smoker.

Many people continue to smoke because they think they will put on lots of weight once they quit. I can only share with you my own ideas and observations on this point. An important role is played by our metabolism. Due to the nicotine in our body, our metabolism operates at an increased speed. It's always working, and the rhythm is higher than that of a nonsmoker.

There are also some other effects, like the increased production of serotonin, which causes additional weight loss or the reduction of body fat levels. Without becoming too scientific, you can say that once you stop smoking, your metabolism slows down again. This allows your body to get much more out of the food you eat. Therefore, gaining a couple of kilograms could be the immediate result of that process, which naturally can vary from one person to another. I put on about five kilos in the beginning. Nothing remarkable. I could only see it when I stood on the scales.

After a while, your body gets used to the new metabolism and your system resets itself. You might lose a few kilos; it varies from person to person. I lost three. From that point on the effect of your old smoking habit is over. Will you eat more when you become a nonsmoker? There is no reason for it. As I described before, it's more a matter of your metabolism resetting itself to normal that causes weight variances.

On the other hand, the food and drink that you'll consume is going to taste twice as good as before! This is one of the amazing revelations

I experienced when I quit. The same food that I had been eating for years became tasty and good again. I realized that I had been missing these wonderful sensations for twenty-five years, only because I was smoking.

The difference is really astonishing. A steak tasted completely different, I could really taste the nice juices of the meat, and I could feel the tomatoes dancing over my tongue. It was a great discovery. I always loved spicy food. When I seasoned my food as I used to when I was a smoker and took the first bite, I thought my head was on fire! I realized I had to cut down on the portions of spicy herbs and oils. And I still love spicy food.

This good taste effect might tempt some of you to eat more for a while after quitting. Consequently, when you eat more, you'll gain some weight. That has nothing to do with smoking. You are just re-gaining the taste skills you lost due to smoking. If you want to reward yourself with this regained skill, that's fine. After all, the most impor-tant thing is that you are a free, happy nonsmoker. This alone deserves a huge celebration.

As you regain your sense of taste, you'll also enjoy sweetness a lot more. This is a common effect once your body is free of nicotine. It's a sweet, strong taste, and a good one. It's wonderful to feel the taste of a piece of chocolate, a nice piece of fresh fruit. You'll be surprised at the difference.

I would certainly advise you to have a small catch-up period. However, as with all other things, don't overdo it, and keep it under con-trol as you did when you were smoking. There is nothing that changes on that side. So there is a good chance that you'll put on some weight. Nothing dramatic, and it can vary from one person to another. Is this a bad thing? No, of course not. You are now a free person who is re-gaining your health and fully enjoying life without any black clouds on your mind. Nobody would even notice that you gained two or three kilos. That's also an illusion caused by another kind of brainwashing in our society.

Most importantly, it all depends on you and how you handle your regained skill of tasting. I can tell you that I love it. I have always loved good food, but today I'm enjoying it so much more. I have become interested in how things taste, what they are, how they are prepared. Cooking is a truly fascinating world.

I would like to say something to my female readers. Since you are reading this book, I assume you are smokers. Whether you are a smoker or a nonsmoker, please share the following idea with your daughters before they decide to reach out for a cigarette.

If your daughter wants to start smoking to control her body weight, tell her that by starting smoking, she is saying this to herself: "Unless I smoke until I die, I'll gain five kilos!" Make sure she fully understands it. Today many young girls start smoking to control their body weight. In fact, all they do is tie themselves to exactly the effect they want to avoid—gaining weight.

Once they have started smoking, they can be absolutely sure that the moment they quit, they will put on some weight, no matter what. If you can convince your daughter of this effect before she starts, there is a good chance she will never start smoking. At least not to control her body weight. Oh, yes, by the way, you are probably curious about my actual weight. Well, it's about six kilos less than when I was a smoker!

᳐

11. Why the solution is easier than you might think

Have you ever wondered what you are afraid of when you think about quitting? Have you ever asked what blocks you from taking one step further? By now you should have asked yourself some pertinent questions. I remember how my brain was going bananas in the months before I finally quit. In my mind, I made the decision to stop smoking. That was a serious thing. That was a big decision I made. I almost immediately backed out of my decision! It was too much for me. It was something I couldn't handle. I thought it wasn't a good time to quit; I would try another time.

Isn't that amazing? I made the decision to stop smoking and then almost immediately decided not to go ahead with it. I came up with hundreds of excuses. Do you recognize this scenario? Have you thought about quitting but immediately changed your mind? I guess, since you are reading this book now, you must have thought about it at least once while buying this book.

If you received the book (*thank* the giver for caring so much about you!), you are having thoughts about quitting since you are still reading. If you are still reading right now, it means that you are serious about your decision to quit. Even if you wander off again, don't panic; there are still enough pages and chapters to put you back on the right track. Let me continue with my story.

When I realized what I was doing, I said to myself that it was crazy. I made a decision and almost immediately backed out of it. Nobody forced me to make that decision, except me. Something forced me to change my mind again. The cigarette dominated me again and controlled my thoughts and decisions. I felt overwhelmed, and then I came up with a solution, I would stick to my decision to stop smoking and start looking for a way to do it without any suffering.

Because that was my biggest fear!!

The fear of suffering, the fear of failure, the fear of having to admit that I was an addict and that this addiction would eventually kill me. The fear of never being able to get rid of cigarettes and my lousy habits. I can assure you, when you smoke about one hundred cigarettes a day, you have a lot to be afraid of; at least that was what I thought.

So I stuck to that decision, and I started my journey to find a way to stop smoking without suffering. The first question I wanted answered was *why* a smoker is so afraid of suffering and failing. I thought if I could find the cause of this fear, it would bring me closer to my solution.

Let me tell you that it wasn't too difficult to find the reason or cause of all these fears. You already know the reason. We discussed it in an earlier chapter. Let us just go over it again so I can explain why these things give you this feeling of fear and disillusion. The main reasons why smokers are afraid to quit are the doctors, the pills and patches, all those antismoking organizations, and most so-called methods for quitting smoking.

Whenever you go to a doctor or a pharmacy, you see posters that say, "Having problems quitting? Ask your doctor for advice, he can help you." "Need help to quit? Ask your doctor for patches and it will be so much easier." You recognize these, don't you? So, what are these phrases telling your brain? Right! They are telling your brain that you can't quit on your own. You need help. You need a *doctor*. Woaah, this must be a serious disease!

If you think you need patches to quit, then you must be worried about what is going to happen when you quit. The fear grows in your mind. This is a good enough reason to continue smoking.

This scared me off like hell. Doctors, not that they don't mean well, completely fail in their attempts, and, even worse, they often create a "believer smoker." This is a smoker who believes he or she has to smoke for the rest of his or her life! Nothing could be further from the truth.

Moreover, there is all the advice you can read or hear from other people, and then there are prescriptions for patches, etc. And they are all telling you how to avoid the pitfalls! Wooah, the *pitfalls!!* They give you advice on what to do when you feel the urge to smoke and think you can't resist it any more. They tell you what to eat and drink so that you'll be able to control your temptation!!

Temptation!

They tell you very clearly that there is a good chance you'll fail! However, the message is "don't worry" and "never give up, it's really worth it." Can you imagine it? Don't panic if you fail, it's fun, just keep going! Have you ever seen a more motivating formula to move people to do something? And this is exactly what this kind of advice does. In your mind, it creates a picture of quitting as something extremely difficult and accompanied by a lot of suffering.

When you look at the patches, they tell you that you have about a 40 percent chance of failure! Give me a break! Personally, I can't believe that these products sell. I have never seen such negative publicity for a product, "When choosing this product, you need to bear in mind that it won't work 40 percent of the time." Come on, let's get serious.

Let me tell you right away, and I'll repeat it many more times, *quitting is the easiest thing you'll ever have to do in your entire life!!!!!!! And you won't suffer a bit!!!!!!!!!!!!*

Do you feel trapped by all that advice? Do you feel misled by the posters in the doctor's office? The problem is, whether you are aware of it or not, they're in your brain and they're working! The good news is that you can get rid of these crazy brainwashing thoughts very easily. Very soon I'll show you and make you realize that *quitting is the easiest thing you'll ever have to do in your entire life!!!!!!! Guaranteed!!!!! And you won't suffer a bit!!!!!*

I guess that by now you have already learned quite a few new things about smoking. Probably things you knew before but didn't look at in this way. As we discussed earlier, fear is one of the biggest obstacles to quitting smoking. We have seen which forms of fear we have and how they are created.

We also saw that most of the things we do or believe in are linked to the pain and pleasure we associate with them. Furthermore, it's a fact that if you question something long enough, you'll start doubting it, even if it's the truth. So, if you believe that you are ready to ask yourself some questions about smoking, you can say that you are on the right path to your liberation.

It doesn't sound too difficult, does it? One of the questions we discussed was what were you missing before you started smoking. I think it's a good moment to reflect on this question again, as a refresher. Ask yourself, "What did I miss before the day I smoked my first cigarette?" Let the question penetrate your thoughts. Let it sink deep into your mind. Maybe you should ask yourself this question before going to sleep. The morning could bring the answer.

Or do you already know the answer? Yes, you do. "Nothing!" Before you started smoking, you missed absolutely nothing at all. How could you? A nonsmoker never misses a cigarette; it's impossible. You probably don't agree. You might think that you really missed something. Everybody else was doing it; they found it cool and good. Only you didn't do it, so you felt alone, etc.

Whatever you are telling yourself is not true. If you have never smoked, you can't miss it; if you did, you would spit it out because it tastes so awful and dull. Since you have been completely brainwashed by heterosuggestions, you might have the illusion of missing something. In reality, you can't miss it, since you don't know it. If you question this issue closely, you'll find the answer.

How can you miss something which your body instinctively reacts to by activating its natural defense mechanism? It doesn't make sense. What did your body do the first time you smoked a cigarette? It made you cough badly; some of you even felt sick! That must be a signal, wouldn't you say?

Could you live with the fact that your body wouldn't give you this signal if it wasn't worthwhile? Yes, why? Because you know that your body will protect you against any possible harm. Asking questions is a natural ability that we human beings have. Asking the right questions and learning from them is much more difficult. That's why so many people have been asking the wrong questions about smoking all their lives. The questions they asked were fed by heterosuggestions and actually led them to start smoking or at least try it.

Now, it's time to reverse the process. It's only by asking the right questions that you'll be able to question your beliefs, your fears, and your illusions. Once you are able to create some serious doubt in your mind concerning these beliefs and illusions, you can change your behavior. Further on I'll guide you through the process of asking good questions about your smoking behavior.

People often underestimate the power of their thoughts and mind in achieving things. Since a lot of things happen to us without us really noticing, we don't count on our mind when we want to make conscious changes in our lives. Our mind is a very powerful tool that will help in the near future. Which person is the best one to help you stop smoking? You often read or hear that it's your doctor. Sometimes you hear that you need your close friends to help and support you. However, the most important person is *you*. You are the only person that can decide whether you'll stop smoking or not and whether you'll succeed or not. Certainly not a doctor, and although I tend to agree that the support of friends is helpful, quite often you'll discover that they work against your success without even realizing it.

This is a consequence of society's heterosuggestion that they were subjected to! These are the people that will probably raise the most doubts and create the most fears during your journey to success, so you'd better know it in advance. This way you can prepare yourself for these events. You'll be able to see through them and put them into perspective.

One of the great advantages of the Painless Stop Smoking Cure is that there are no difficult moments. This might sound unbelievable to you at this moment, but you'll understand it while you learn more about this down-to-earth method. Since it's a mental process that you need to go through, under conditions as they are right now, you are going to miss absolutely nothing.

There is no reason to be nervous; there is no place for withdrawal pains, and no reason to panic or feel bad. You'll become a free, happy nonsmoker even before smoking your last cigarette. The moment you become free and experience your Final Liberation, you'll usually still be smoking. This allows you to quit without any negative side effects whatsoever. You'll be able to celebrate your great victory and finally enjoy your regained freedom.

Another benefit is that any type of a smoker can use this method. It makes no difference whether you are a heavy chain smoker or an occasional or social smoker. The method works the same for men and women. Every person will experience and apply the method at his own pace. Nobody can determine what will work best for you. Remember this well.

Nobody and nothing, not even this book, can make this decision for you. This is totally up to you. Naturally, this book will guide you through the process, but in the end, only you can decide whether and when you are ready for the next step.

Some of you might be thinking that this method won't work, in the same way as everything else you tried. Well, let me be very honest with you here. If you truly believe this won't work, it won't! Simple! As I said earlier, the success of this method depends entirely on you. The first and main tool for succeeding with the Painless Stop Smoking Cure is your belief—your belief in yourself. No, not willpower. Just the fact that you believe in yourself and your own destiny. When you tell yourself beforehand that something won't work out, whether it's quitting smoking or anything else, it won't work out. You have programmed yourself for defeat.

So, if you have already tried several other things, let me first congratulate you!! You are at least trying to do something to liberate yourself from nicotine. You have already proven that you are not afraid of trying things. You have proven that you don't know failure, since the only failure that exists is giving up trying. The difference now is that you are not going to try to do something; you are just going to do it! Yes, you read that correctly; this method doesn't even allow trying. You do it and you succeed or you don't. You can't just try it! This is the biggest benefit of the method! When you apply it, it works. If you don't apply it, it doesn't. It's guaranteed!

So, you can relax now. There is nothing to worry about; you are going to succeed! Period. One of the main characteristics of the Painless Stop Smoking Cure is the fact that millions of people have already used it to quit. One day they decided to stop smoking (not to "give up" smoking; remember, there is nothing to "give up"), and they just did it. They quit, didn't suffer a bit, and never ever smoked again. Right. How many people do you know that quit like that? Think about it. Yeah, you are amazed, aren't you? When you start thinking about it, you suddenly find examples of quite a few people who quit "just like that." How come you didn't think of those people earlier? Because they are not a part of heterosuggestion brainwashing.

I remember one day when I was coming back from a visit to a client in the Ardennes, I picked up a hitchhiker. He was a guy a few years older than me. He worked in the construction business. I could see and smell that he had gone to a big party the night before. He told me he "lost" his car and thus he had to hitchhike home. During our trip, he heard me coughing. He could guess the cause when I asked him if it was OK if I smoked. "I'm bothered for you; I couldn't care less," he said. Woah! What an answer. He told me he used to smoke two packs a day. One day he had a heavy cold and started to cough for several weeks.

Then he decided that he was tired of it. He had enough, and he stopped smoking, just like that. No withdrawal pains, no desire to smoke, no need for nicotine. He just quit. He became a happy, free nonsmoker in a split second. I remember how jealous I was as he told me his story. I envied him deep inside my heart. "How did you do it?" I asked. He didn't know. It just happened; it was so easy. How many stories do you know like this? How many stories like this have you heard? Thousands of people quit exactly this way. The only problem for you is that they don't know how it happened and therefore they can't explain it to you.

What we are doing together right now is exactly that. You are learning and discovering step by step how they did it—how I did it. That is the Painless Stop Smoking Cure that so many people have applied to quitting without even realizing. That's my message to you. Nothing more, nothing less. Quite simple, wouldn't you agree?

Meanwhile you and I have already done a part of the journey, and as a result, you already know more than you actually think you do. This is a part of the Painless Stop Smoking Cure. It is the same for the results. Sometimes people wonder how they will know whether they succeeded or not.

How can we know?

With the Painless Stop Smoking Cure, it's very simple. You'll know it before you smoke your last cigarette! This is why I told you that you can't fail. Before you smoke your last cigarette, you'll have become a free, happy nonsmoker. Your last cigarette is just a ritual to bury your past slavery. Before I get you even more confused, let's have a short look at a great powerful partner that will accompany you on your journey—your subconscious mind.

❧

12. How can your subconscious mind be your best friend or your biggest enemy?

Although I don't want to go into too much detail here, I believe it's crucial we go through some material about our mind. This is necessary to understand its role and influence on our behavior. I presume most of you have heard about the subconscious mind, but what is it? What is our mind? What is our mind composed of?

First of all, your mind is the most precious and powerful possession you have. It's always with you, and you just have to learn how to make the best of its enormous powers. Our mind is split into two parts, a conscious part and an unconscious or subconscious part. Often it's presented as the conscious mind lying above the unconscious; this is where the name subconscious mind is derived from. Your conscious mind is the mind you think with; it's your reasoning mind. You make all your decisions with your conscious mind.

Your subconscious mind is the home of your emotions. It's your creative mind. If you think good, good will follow; if you think evil, evil will follow. Once your subconscious mind accepts an idea, it begins to execute it. What you consciously think with your conscious mind will sink down to your subconscious mind. Whatever you feel is true; your subconscious mind will accept it and turn it into your experience. Your subconscious mind accepts what your conscious mind believes in.

Your subconscious mind accepts all kinds of suggestions, good and false. These suggestions can be very powerful, and we have all had several experiences with them.

If, for example, you have to wake up at a certain time for an important meeting or event, don't you wake up just on time? Try it. Let's say you have to wake up tomorrow at 7 a.m. Don't set your alarm clock. When you go to bed, just think strongly about the fact that you absolutely have to wake up at seven. Go to sleep. You'll see that you'll wake up at 7 a.m.! That's an example of the true power of your subconscious mind.

Have you ever bought a new car? Or have you ever changed from one model to another? What happened? What did you notice in the streets? Isn't it strange that the moment you have changed to your new Ford, you suddenly notice a lot more Ford cars? Or when you set your mind on a Harley Davidson, you suddenly see a lot more Harleys passing by? There are still as many Fords or Harleys in your neighborhood as before; it's the power of your subconscious mind that makes you notice them more.

The danger is that your subconscious mind can't reason. It reacts to the impressions and suggestions given by your conscious mind. That is why you have to know how to handle it, so it becomes your partner instead of your enemy.

Because people have different beliefs, they react differently to the same suggestions. Take an experienced marine, for example. If you walked up to him while on a cruise and told him he was looking a little bit pale and might get seasick, what would happen? Would he really become seasick? What if you tried the same suggestion on a young man or woman who was traveling at sea for the first time and is impressed with the huge ocean and the movement of the ship? Depending on what their beliefs are, the suggestion will or will not have an effect.

As you have seen, you have different beliefs, fears, and illusions about smoking. These inner assumptions rule your behavior. A suggestion itself has no power. Its power comes from the fact that you accept it mentally. The moment you believe something, you don't question it anymore. Therefore, it's important to question the beliefs you have about smoking. The moment you start to question your beliefs, you start to lose the certainty you have about them. The ground on which your beliefs are based starts shaking as you start questioning their references. The stronger the beliefs, and thus the references, the deeper questions you have to ask yourself.

There are two types of suggestion. One suggestion we already discussed: the heterosuggestions. These are suggestions coming from other people. As we have seen, and as you have experienced, these heterosuggestions can be very powerful. The process of heterosuggestion starts the moment you are born. It involves all aspects of your life; beliefs, politics, education, culture, etc.

Autosuggestion is a specific suggestion one gives to oneself. It can be positive or negative. You will remember what I said earlier that if you belief something won't work, it won't. This is a clear example of a negative autosuggestion. You suggest to yourself that something is not going to work before you try to do it. Your subconscious mind can't make distinctions, so it starts to project what has been suggested to it. The actual result will be the same as the suggestion sent to your subconscious mind. Your subconscious mind will respond accordingly.

With your conscious mind, you can decide what you are going to suggest to your subconscious mind. This is why you have to pay attention to the thoughts you have. We have already discussed most of the thoughts, fears, and beliefs you, a smoker, have about smoking. These have been given to your subconscious mind, which accepts them as true and acts accordingly.

So if you believe that quitting is difficult, guess what? It's difficult! Your subconscious mind will make you feel that it's difficult to stop smoking. Your subconscious mind is very powerful, and you won't be able to change the way it perceive things with another thought of your conscious mind. You can try, but it won't work. That is what people who stop smoking using the willpower method experience.

They want to quit, they quit; however, their subconscious mind is constantly reminding them what they believe in, that it's difficult to quit. They fight it with their conscious mind and make the decision not to smoke, not to give in, by confirming and empowering the suggestion that it's hard to stop smoking. The subconscious mind is usually the winner.

You can guide your subconscious mind by choosing what to believe in with your conscious mind. Therefore, you need to pay attention to what you say, think, and believe in. From now on, start questioning the belief that quitting is difficult. Go back to the chapter where we discussed it and let those questions penetrate your mind. It will bring you another step closer to your Final Liberation.

Remember that whatever your conscious mind assumes or believes to be true, your subconscious mind will accept and bring to life. Your subconscious mind controls all the vital processes and functions of your body. Your subconscious mind never sleeps and is always open to suggestion. Whatever thoughts, beliefs or illusions on smoking you pass to your subconscious mind, you'll experience them as circumstances, conditions, and events.

This is how our mind functions and influences our lives on a daily basis. If you consciously think that it's very difficult to stop smoking that is exactly how you'll feel about it. If you believe that cigarettes help you when you are stressed, nervous, bored, or lazy, that's how you'll feel.

In previous chapters, you and I started to look at beliefs and illusions about smoking from a different point of view. The reason we did that was to start your questioning process. Don't worry whether this process has started or not; it has started even if you are not fully aware of it. While you are reading these chapters and thinking about the words and questions, some of the information leaks through to your subconscious mind. Since your subconscious mind can't judge, it doesn't select the questions, it just tries to answer them. Some people will already be further on in this process than others will. From time to time, you might want to reread the chapters you still have doubts about. This will help your mind to keep asking these questions.

By continuously asking these questions, you'll slowly but certainly destabilize your beliefs and illusions. Suggestions have been proven to be the best way to communicate with your subconscious mind. Advertising agents know this very well. That's why they use so many suggestions in their advertisements, like the suggestions of freedom, stardom, adventure, being in control, etc.

All publicity of cigarettes is based on deeper suggestions. Why? Because it's difficult to promote just the "taste" of a cigarette. That wouldn't be a big success. It only becomes a success by linking the cigarette to a deeper suggestion. Publicity attributes positive emotions to advertised objects. Therefore, every time you see or use the object, you experience this positive emotion. Your subconscious mind will help you get these emotions and thus direct your conscious mind to make a choice of brand A and not B.

If you want to communicate with your subconscious mind, you can best do it when your conscious mind is less active. In this way, you can better direct the information you want to get through to your subconscious mind. One of the easiest ways to communicate is visualization. You try to get a clear picture of what you want; you try to see it clearly before you, with shapes and colors, etc. Athletes try to visualize themselves crossing the finish line first. They can hear the applause of the public; they can see the gold medal hanging on their chest.

When you are lying in bed, just about to fall asleep, try visualizing what you want. Can you imagine what it would be like if you were a free, happy nonsmoker? How would you start your day? What things would you do differently? Is it possible for you to picture yourself as a nonsmoker, or are the beliefs and illusions you have still too strong? Close your eyes for a while and try to see a picture of yourself as a non-smoker. Take a common situation when you would normally smoke— for example, in your car, in front of the television, or waiting for a train or a bus. First take a look at yourself with a cigarette. What do you do? What is the sequence of actions you do? How do you feel? Are you cold or are you warm? Do you have a cough? If there are people around you, how do they react?

Now, take the same situation, but remove the cigarette. What happens? Do you panic? How do you feel now? What are the things you do instead? Does it make you feel different? Do you still have a cough? How do the people around you react? Did you like what you saw or not? Maybe you were still not able to see yourself as a nonsmoker, or maybe you panicked. That's fine. This is of secondary importance. The important thing is that you are making progress.

It's important that you understand how your subconscious mind works and how you can use its enormous power to your advantage. You must remember that whenever your subconscious mind accepts an idea, it immediately begins to execute it. This rule applies not only to good ideas, but to bad ones as well.

In order to overcome failure, you have to get your subconscious mind to accept your ideas and requests. Feel its reality now and the law of your mind will do the rest. Turn over your request with faith and confidence, and your subconscious mind will take over and bring you the results. Failure is inevitable when you make statements like, "It's hopeless." "I see no way out." "This will never work." "I don't know what to do." Making statements like this won't help you get any further. You can only wait and observe as they become reality!

To better communicate with your subconscious mind, you need to keep your conscious mind out of it. Why? When you try to visualize yourself as a free, happy non-smoker, your conscious mind will try to get in the way; it will try to give you answers and solve the issue. This will then be passed on to the subconscious mind. Resist this. Let your problem-solving skills go to sleep. Picture yourself as a happy, free nonsmoker. Imagine the emotional gratification of the freedom state you would be in. Remember that your imagination is a very powerful source. Imagine the end result in front of you.

Detach yourself from your conscious mind. Just imagine, see, and feel the joy, the power, and the freedom of being a free, happy nonsmoker. Imagine that you have to walk on a narrow plank that is lying on the floor; you wouldn't have a problem with this, would you? It would be easy to do. Now imagine that we put the plank ten meters high; would you still walk on the plank? Probably not. Your desire to walk on the plank is in conflict with your imagination. You are imagining yourself falling down to the ground. You might want to walk along the plank, but your fear of falling down would keep you from doing it.

It's exactly the same with smoking. You have the desire to quit, but your imagination, brainwashed by all those heterosuggestions, is so afraid of the consequences of quitting that you can't succeed. The harder you try, the higher your chance of failure. You can't suppress your imagination. The more you do this, the more strength you give to the idea of fear. The idea that you'll use your willpower to overcome your failure reinforces the thought of failure.

In case this is not clear, let's do a short exercise. I am now going to ask you *not* to think about a big green frog. Ribbit, ribbit. What are you thinking about? You are thinking about a frog. The harder you try not to think about the frog, the bigger and clearer the picture will become in your mind. This is how the power of the subconscious mind works.

A lot of people who want to stop smoking are trying too hard, and that is the exact reason why they don't succeed. The solution is to align the conscious and subconscious minds in the first place and avoid any conflict between the two by approaching your subconscious mind while you are almost asleep. Imagine the fulfillment of being a free, happy nonsmoker over and over again before falling asleep. It will work miracles.

Is there anything you have noticed so far while reading this book? Is there anything that you find different from other books or texts you have read about smoking? Well, I'll tell you. What is the purpose of this book? "That's easy," I hear you say, "to stop smoking!" Well, *no!* That is *not* the purpose of this book; it will be the result of this book.

The purpose of this book is for you to become a free, happy nonsmoker. Is there a difference? Yes, a very big difference! Think again about our frog. You got it.

The purpose of this book is for you to become a free, happy non-smoker. This implies that you'll have no desire to smoke. There will be no more need for a cigarette. You'll understand that a cigarette can give you absolutely nothing. I don't care that you want to stop smoking. I know that! Otherwise you wouldn't be reading this book. I want you to remove your desire to smoke and all the other illusions that make you smoke. If you succeed in achieving that, guess what? You won't smoke ever again!!

Many people who want to become free, happy nonsmokers focus on the fact that they want to stop smoking. They want to quit doing something. So what happens? Nothing. Imagine you stopped doing it; what would happen? You don't know. You stop smoking. Great. But what is really happening? You become a free, happy non-smoker. That is what is happening. You're going from one state to another state. You can't just stay in between.

This is very important to understand.

When you want to change something, you have to know the outcome, and you have to replace the past with a new state. A pleasant state. A great state. As you remember, we are driven by what we link pain and pleasure to. Therefore, you have to visualize yourself as a free, happy nonsmoker with all the possible great, positive feelings and effects. Your drive towards this new pleasure will be much greater than your drive towards the old, painful, enslaving situation you were in.

You can now see through the illusions of nicotine, and you'll no longer tolerate the stupid thoughts that made you a slave to nicotine for so many years. You now understand that you want to be free! You want to fully enjoy every aspect of your life. You want to smell and taste things with full intensity. You want to walk around without worrying about where your cigarettes are. You have no more desire for cigarettes.

So you have to focus on the affirmative. Focusing on ideas like "I want to stop smoking" introduces a negative idea to your subconscious, like "stop thinking about that frog." Becoming a free, happy nonsmoker is an affirmative idea. You should see this as clearly as possible. Your subconscious mind will magnify whatever you suggest to it. What I mean is that whatever you suggest to your subconscious mind, it will add something to it—something positive when your message is positive, something negative when it's negative. Remember that your subconscious mind can't reason.

To look at it from another angle, consider your conscious mind as a camera and your subconscious mind as the sensitive plate on which the picture is registered. No matter what picture you take, it will be registered on the sensitive plate. This shows why it's so important to create a detailed, specific picture of it. With your conscious mind, you can focus on things just like the camera. Once you have focused, there is nothing else you can do. Therefore, there is no reason to struggle. Let your subconscious mind develop the picture you focus on. All you can do is guide your thoughts and focus your attention on the picture you have of yourself as a free, happy nonsmoker.

I want to thank those who are still with me. This wasn't the easiest chapter, I know. Maybe you would like to reread it for deeper understanding. Although it's not necessary to fully understand how your mind works, I consider this an extra tool for your journey to your Final Liberation. Let's now have a look at what the Painless Stop Smoking Cure is all about. You'll see that there is nothing airy fairy about it; it's all common sense.

&

13. The Painless Stop Smoking Cure, plain common sense, and belief in oneself

By now, I believe you must have a good feeling about the process you are involved in. Therefore, it's time to go a little bit deeper into this process to speed up your Final Liberation.

When you bought this book, you bought it because somewhere in your mind you were considering quitting smoking. You had the wish to stop smoking. That is good, and actually, it's also the first step in the overall process. If you received this book from a friend or relative, I would thank this person. It's a sign that they care for you very much and wish you all the best. In that case, you probably didn't think about quitting before, and you started reading the book out of curiosity. I bet you have changed your mind in the meanwhile.

Your mental attitude, your desire, and your determination are of key importance in whether you succeed or not. If you don't want to stop smoking, don't even bother; it won't work. Bear in mind though that I'm not asking you to be convinced that you'll stop smoking. All I'm asking is that you have the desire to stop smoking. Most of you have this desire at this moment. This is good and bad.

That is why I'm going to ask you, as I mentioned before, to give up this desire and replace it with a new one. This new desire is to become a free, happy nonsmoker. Is this clear to you? Can you do this? You want to become a free, happy nonsmoker. That's all. Now I want you to desire this very strongly. You truly want to become a free, happy nonsmoker. There is nothing that can stop you from continuing your journey towards it. You'll feel strong enough to overcome any obstacles you encounter on your way. You *absolutely* want and will become a free, happy nonsmoker.

That is all I'm asking of you. Most of you will have no problem with this. You'll also understand why this change in desire is necessary. Some of you might still be in doubt. Why are you in doubt? Because of your fears and illusions.

Reading this book may have removed some of your fears and illusions, but probably not all of them. Everybody has to go through this process at his or her own speed. Before you do so, I want you to create the desire to become a free, happy nonsmoker.

Those of you who are afraid are thinking of the consequences. It's all right to think about them, but only in this very moment, then forget about the consequences. Remember what we've already said: it's not always the pain alone that drives us to do or not to do things, but also the fear that doing something will lead to pain.

Fear is nothing but the work of your mind. So, when you fear something, you are actually afraid of your own thoughts. Frequently these fears don't exist in real life. They have no reality. But for now, just try to see yourself as a free, happy nonsmoker, and don't worry about the way you'll make it happen. Just imagine that you clap your hands and become a free, happy nonsmoker in an instant!

Do you want it? Do you have the desire for this to happen? To become a free, happy nonsmoker in a split second without suffering a bit? I guess everybody would want this. Just think about this. Picture it very clearly in your mind. What does it look like? What does it feel like?

Don't think about the *how*!

Just think about the fact and think about the why. Why will you be a free, happy nonsmoker? Think about this. Let it play in your mind. Decide today that you *absolutely* desire to become a free, happy non-smoker. Of course, you can keep on smoking; I even want you to. Smoke as much as you want, but decide today that you absolutely want to become a free, happy nonsmoker, regardless of what it will take. That is another step.

Are you there? Have you taken the decision that *you absolutely desire to become a free, happy nonsmoker*? Are you absolutely sure? Are there still doubts in your mind about what you want? No, not the *how*, just the fact of being a nonsmoker. Imagine you can't fail; do you desire to become a free, happy nonsmoker? I want to hear *yes!* I want to hear a very loud *yes*. I want you to scream out as loud as you can: *yes!!!*

After reading this paragraph, I want you to put this book away and walk to a big mirror. Now, I want you to look deep into your own eyes, really deep.

Now, I want you to shout out, with all the joy and energy you have, *"I absolutely want to be a free, happy nonsmoker!" "I absolutely want to be a free, happy nonsmoker!!!"*

Louder, give it some more energy.

Go on! I want you to shout it out loud at least five times.

And keep watching yourself in the mirror. Feel and observe how the joy rises in your body. Feel how you are filled with energy. Now go to that mirror and shout out loud!! Are you back?

Does it feel good?!!

Yeah, I bet it does!! OK! Can you feel this warm glow? Great. If, at this moment you don't have the *absolute desire* to be a free, happy nonsmoker, please *don't read any further!*

This is crucial. If you don't have the desire to become a free, happy nonsmoker, reread the beginning of this chapter, reread all the previous chapters, but don't continue, as it won't help you any further. There is no reason to panic; just go back to some chapters, let the questions sink into your mind, and I'm sure I'll see you back in no time. Are you there? *Congratulations!*

I have some very good news for you. You have completed more than half of your journey to your Final Liberation! Isn't this great news? You are already more than 50 percent a free, happy nonsmoker! I think you should celebrate this, don't you agree? Some of you might wonder what is so great about it, since that's exactly what you wanted from the very beginning.

The reason why it's such great news is that you have just created a picture of your desired outcome. As you know, your subconscious mind is very powerful and brings out what you imprint on it. Now it's just a matter of a gradual process that has been started. To be quite honest with you, this process started at the very beginning of this book. However, back then you might not have been receptive to it; that's why I'm only mentioning it now.

You have just achieved yet another thing which I didn't mention earlier: you admitted you are a drug addict. How did you do this? By desiring to become "free." This implied to your mind that you are not free at the moment, which is true, since you are a prisoner, a slave to nicotine. Fantastic! I'm sure you feel the same and can't wait to go on.

However, I want you to stop for a moment. I want to remind you that it's not a race against time. It really doesn't matter whether you become a free, happy nonsmoker in two days, two weeks, or two months. Or does it? What I consider most important is the fact that you'll become a free, happy nonsmoker. Without suffering and in an instant! Some of you may already have the feeling of the big Final Liberation, and that's great. You can already smoke your last cigarette and be through with it.

Most of you still need more time and have to continue reading. I hope you'll agree with me that the most important thing is for you to become a *free, happy nonsmoker* in a short while, without suffering, without withdrawal pains, without willpower or other fantasies.

Let's go one step further now, before I go into some more detail about the Painless Stop Smoking Cure. There is nothing special about it; it's all common sense. The problem is that nobody ever guided you through this process before. You now have a deep desire. If you close your eyes, what does this desire look like?

What great feelings do you experience? Do you feel the energy flowing through your body? Could you scream out loud from joy and happiness? What do you feel about yourself? How proud are you? Do you feel that your confidence is stronger? Can you rule the world? Do you have a very clear picture of what you see, what you feel, what you enjoy. Do you like the picture of your new self? What is your partner saying about you? How does it feel to be free? Hold this picture for a while, with these feelings, and enjoy the moment.

I know that some of you still have doubts; others will still have fears. Remember, fear is not a reality. Fear is just a warning signal telling us to prepare for what is about to happen. You are doing this, step by step. That's why the fear may appear from time to time. Every time fears or doubts come up, I want you to go back to the picture you have just created. The clear picture of yourself as a free, happy nonsmoker. See and feel this picture and let it sink into your subconscious mind. This is the condition you *absolutely* desire to achieve. You can feel it, as if it's a reality.

Let's talk about your remaining fears and how to overcome them. I told you that we are halfway through, right? Did you feel anything? Did you feel bad at any moment? Did I hurt you? Good, so I won't hurt you during the remaining part of our journey together! The next thing I want you to do won't be too difficult, if you pay careful attention to what I say.

You have the *absolute desire to be a free, happy nonsmoker.* We agree on this, right? I urged you not to think about the *how* but only about the *why.* For the next step of the process, I want you to completely forget and exclude all possible thoughts, ideas, doubts, and fears you might still have about the *how.* Just forget about them. Imagine there is no *how.* Imagine there is only "a moment"—a moment in which you *are* a free, happy nonsmoker.

Can you do this?

Imagine that it's not possible for you to suffer, or fail; there is only the result. You only need to focus on the outcome, on the result, and you'll be there, just like that. You'll have no idea how you found yourself in the situation. You'll become a free, happy nonsmoker. You don't feel any desire for cigarettes or nicotine anymore. You don't want to smoke. You can't think of one good thing that a cigarette could do for you. Good.

Now I want you to make a decision. I want you to make a very strong, irreversible decision. You know which decision? Great. I want you to concentrate totally on the picture of yourself as a free, happy nonsmoker who has no desire for cigarettes or nicotine. I want you to decide that this is what you'll become.

You'll decide right now that you'll be a free, happy nonsmoker.

Make this decision right now, knowing that when you make a true decision, there is no turning back. You eliminate all other possibilities. It's that simple. You decide and promise yourself that you'll become a free, happy nonsmoker. And as you make this decision, focus on your picture where you are already a free, happy nonsmoker. Go back in front of the mirror now and look yourself in the eyes. Feel good about yourself, feel proud, and promise yourself, "I'll be a free, happy nonsmoker!"

Check and rehearse your decision again: "I'll be a free, happy nonsmoker!" Great; remember that you have now made a true decision. You hereby eliminated all other possibilities. This means you have to become a free, happy nonsmoker. Isn't this great? Isn't such a strong decision like this empowering?

I remember the moment I made this decision for myself. I was sitting in my hotel room in Copenhagen. The room was made of 80 percent wood. It was typical for Denmark, but here it was especially nice. I had a beautiful view of a small river passing through the capital, and the sun had just fallen behind the horizon.

So I was staring through the window when I suddenly asked myself the question, why did I continue to smoke? Immediately I came up with the classic excuses, the illusions. I panicked and wanted to think about something else. I have no idea why, but my mind held on to the idea of quitting. So I asked myself another question: "Eric, do you want to stop smoking?" I was thinking about it, but answering seemed difficult. I couldn't answer the question. So I asked myself another question: "Eric, do you want to go back to the moment before you smoked your first cigarette?" That was an easy one: "Yes, of course." I wouldn't be a nicotine addict, I wouldn't suffer from withdrawal pains, I wouldn't have the need or desire for a cigarette. I asked, "Eric, would you like to get rid of the desire for cigarettes?" Yes, that was it. That was my chance. If I could remove my desire, my need for cigarettes, there would be no reason left to keep on smoking. Moreover, since I wouldn't have the desire anymore, I wouldn't suffer either. Therefore, I promised myself that I would become a free, happy nonsmoker. I made a decision that I couldn't turn away from. At least not if I still wanted to look myself in the eye.

The immediate consequence of this decision was that I had to find a way to stop smoking without suffering. My fear of pain is very high, and it had prevented me from taking such a decision for years. Now the decision was made. There was no turning back. I had to succeed!! I felt very satisfied, and I was proud of myself for having made such a big decision. All I had to do was to find a way to stop smoking without suffering. The journey began…

Therefore, here we are, you and I. We have both taken the same decision for Final Liberation. Your advantage, however, is that you don't have to look for a way to stop smoking without suffering. You are already using it, and you are more than halfway through. Isn't that fantastic?

So, now you must be curious to find out exactly what this Painless Stop Smoking Cure consists of. Don't you want to know how this method is going to work for you? Well, I won't keep you waiting any longer. Let us quickly go over the concept without losing too much time. We have more serious work to do.

As you have already discovered by now, the fact that you are a smoker and the fact that you *still* are a smoker are the consequences of suggestions that are made to our mind: heterosuggestions made by society, friends, and relatives, autosuggestions made by yourself, and the balloon suggestions made by nicotine. By frequent repetition and by certain reference criteria, these suggestions become beliefs, fears, and illusions you have about cigarettes and smoking.

So, if this is the original cause for you to be a smoker, a nicotine addict, if this creates your desire for a cigarette, what can possibly stop it?

Exactly, suggestions!

Your suggestions, powerful suggestions you'll send to your mind. This will allow your subconscious mind to build new, empowering beliefs that will guide you and finally set you free. These new beliefs will destroy all the references, all the criteria, the old illusions and fears. Once your new empowering beliefs have destroyed the old ones, you'll become *free!* Let me tell you that at this very moment, you have already replaced quite a few old beliefs. More than you might think.

Of course, this will vary from person to person. However, if you are still reading, you have made enormous progress. You can count on your subconscious mind to guide you to Final Liberation.

Is that it now?

Of course not.

I won't leave you alone like this. Let's have a quick look at the acronym I found for the Painless Stop Smoking Cure. Then we will look at how to put things into practice.

This is exactly what you are already doing.

As I mentioned before it's a gradual process that everyone has to go through at their pace. Nobody can force you or your subconscious mind. When you try, you will only get the reverse effect. Remember this. Don't forget the two major steps you took while reading this chapter. You created the *desire* to become a free, happy nonsmoker, and you made the *decision* to become a free, happy nonsmoker. Yes, unconditionally. No worries, no stress, no withdrawals, no fears, nothing. You achieved a great thing. The fact that you are still with me means that you are going to succeed.

By the way, let me remind you of the fact that you can only succeed!! Please, consider this very carefully: you can only succeed with the Painless Stop Smoking Cure. There is no other alternative. You don't stop smoking to find out later that you still want a cigarette.

No, you smoke and find out that you don't want a cigarette anymore! That's how it works. Bear that in mind and don't allow yourself to become frightened by any other thoughts, suggestions, or anything else that may put your mind back on the old track. You are now wondering how you can create such autosuggestions to help you on your journey. There are many suggestions that have been given to you throughout this book.

It will do no harm to reread the first chapters. It will only help and improve your mind-set to create the right pictures and beliefs for your subconscious mind.

In the next chapters, you are going to learn how you can create and install powerful suggestions in your mind. You'll find out that it's an easy and natural process. It's just a matter of which questions you ask, and there are just three questions to ask.

But first, you and I are going to determine your moment of Final Liberation…

↷

14. How to choose your moment of Final Liberation

We have come a long way together, haven't we? The last two chapters were not easy, do you agree? They may even seem a little bizarre to some of you. If this is the case, no problem. It's actually quite logical that these topics create question marks in your mind.

Why?

Well, on the one hand, these are not topics we talk about on a daily basis, while on the other hand, they are constantly present in our minds. They have an enormous influence on how we do things and how we perceive the world around us. Most people never look closely at topics like these. When you are then confronted with them, they may sound strange or look bizarre. They make you feel a bit uncomfortable, right?

Why don't we have a look at how you can make use of these topics in your daily life? How can you put these things into practice? First, let us go back to our desire to be a free, happy nonsmoker. Recall that picture you created of yourself. Close your eyes and see all the things you'll experience as a free, happy nonsmoker.

Are you there?

Good. It's important that you keep this vivid picture in front of you as often as possible. I am not asking you to walk around all day with only this picture in your mind. What I am asking or advising you to do is very simple. Every morning before you get up and every night just before you fall asleep, recall this picture and enjoy the views and feelings it gives you. It's important that from now on you see yourself as a free, happy nonsmoker. I want you to confront yourself with this new *you* on a daily basis.

The more frequently you see yourself as a free, happy nonsmoker, the easier it becomes to associate yourself with this picture, with this image. Your subconscious mind will be fully impressed with this new image and will start turning it into reality.

There is another reason you absolutely should do this. As a smoker, you have all the illusions, beliefs, and fears caused by heterosuggestions and the balloon effect. When you picture yourself as a free, happy nonsmoker, you start to realize that these illusions, beliefs, and fears are most likely not right. You start to see through them. You start to create new beliefs. You can't force this; neither can I. I can't tell you which belief you'll have to create. I don't know which fear will disappear first. You're the only person who has any influence on it. And even then, I don't want you to force it. Let it take its natural course. If you focus regularly on the new image of yourself as a free, happy nonsmoker, it will come. It's a gradual process.

You didn't only create a desire to be a free, happy nonsmoker; you went much further. You made *the decision* to be a free, happy nonsmoker! This is a great breakthrough—probably the biggest breakthrough you have ever made as a smoker. You actually made the decision to stop smoking. You know that we say it differently; you made the decision to free yourself from the need for cigarettes and nicotine. No more desire for cigarettes.

Why is it so important?

It's a decision that you made as a free person without being forced to do so. It's a promise you made to yourself. A true decision that rules out all other possibilities. There is no other way. No turning back. You don't get into a panic anymore, since you have learned that the Painless Stop Smoking Cure guarantees that there will be no suffering involved. That is correct—no suffering at all, just the great feeling the moment after you have smoked your last cigarette and all the moments thereafter.

You know that with the Painless Stop Smoking Cure, you actually continue to smoke until you reach your Final Liberation. Until that time, you can't suffer from withdrawal pains or any other bad feelings. You already know that these don't really exist, but I'll repeat it in case you are not completely sure of it yet.

The moment you smoke your last cigarette, you'll already be free of all illusions, all the beliefs and fears you ever had about smoking and especially about quitting. By that time, you'll have created new, strong beliefs about the truth about smoking. You won't have any desire for nicotine or cigarettes anymore. And all this, because today you made this marvelous decision!

What I would like to ask you now is to add just a very small thing to this great decision. You made this great decision to be a free, happy nonsmoker. All that is missing is for you to determine by when you want to be a free, happy nonsmoker. I can understand that some of you might say, "Now!" and that is OK. Some of you can achieve it at this stage. Congratulations! The majority of us will have to choose a longer deadline. Let me give you some advice on this.

When I made the decision to be a free, happy nonsmoker, I linked it with the fact that I had to find a way to quit without suffering for a split second. While I was figuring out how it could work, I realized that I couldn't spend my entire life trying to find a way. I needed a sense of urgency. I needed something to "torture" my brains a bit.

Therefore, I gave myself three months to find the way and carry it through to become a free, happy nonsmoker. It actually took me about two months to find the way and put it into practice. What a revelation it was when I could finally see through it all! It was one of the most amazing moments in my life.

Now, you probably think that you have an easier path to follow since I'm going to tell you the way. So you might think you can become a free, happy nonsmoker within a week or a couple of days. Maybe. That depends on you. By the way, you have been on the path to success and freedom from the very first moment you started reading this book.

Therefore, it's possible that you'll get to your moment of Final Liberation faster than I did. That would be fine. However, as mentioned before, timing is not that important. It's important but there are other things of greater importance that can provide you with a lot more support. When the moment of your Final Liberation comes, it will only take a split second to change from a smoker to a non-smoker. Amazing, isn't it? Just a split second to achieve something you wanted for so long but were so afraid of. And it will happen to you. As you read on, this fantastic moment is getting closer and closer.

Maybe what I'm going to tell you right now will shock you at first. Please, read on so you understand what I mean. The Painless Stop Smoking Cure won't show you the path you have to take until you reach Final Liberation. No, simply because it's impossible. Woah! I can hear some of you react! Listen. The Painless Stop Smoking Cure will "guide" you on your path to your Final Liberation.

What does that mean?

It means just what it says. Firstly, it means that, yes, there certainly is a path; secondly, that you'll reach your moment of Final Liberation; and thirdly, that you'll be guided all the way until you succeed. Isn't that what you really want? Isn't that the best support you can expect?

Look at so many other methods which give you the path. What kind of methods are these anyway? Take these pills every day for sixty days. Remove all objects related to cigarettes from your home. When you stop smoking, drink a lot of water. Don't eat red meat. Don't go to bars or places where people smoke. Don't drink alcohol. Avoid people that smoke.

Think of something else when you want to smoke. Wear a patch on your chest for thirty days. Ask your doctor how to quit; he knows how difficult it is. And so on. Do you want more of this BS or what? None of these methods work! And you know it better than anyone else. You have probably tried some of them!

The Painless Stop Smoking Cure is going to be your guide, your partner, while you are traveling to a well-defined destination—your moment of Final Liberation, the moment you become a free, happy nonsmoker. Every time you intend to leave your path, there is your guide and partner steering you in the right direction. This way you can be sure that you'll arrive at your destination at the time you predicted.

So we are back to the issue of choosing a deadline. There is one golden rule here. Don't read on beyond this chapter unless you have decided on your deadline and written it down in your journal or on a piece of paper to confirm it to yourself. Otherwise it won't work. It's of key importance that you know the outcome in advance! You already have the picture; you know the feelings and emotions of being a free, happy nonsmoker. Now you still need to add the moment of your Final Liberation. Let me help you.

The moment you choose will be the ultimate deadline in achieving your goal. Almost certainly, you'll attain it much sooner. So, once you have your deadline set, don't focus on it too much. Moreover, provide enough time for your mind to work. Everything depends on two major things: firstly, how deeply you have been brainwashed by the hetero-suggestions and the balloon effect, and secondly, how easily you can let your autosuggestions work for you. Some of you will become free, happy nonsmokers before finishing this book; others may already be there. This is because you can put so much power into these newly gained suggestions that you destroy all other illusions, beliefs, and fears. Once that happens, it's over; you are a free, happy nonsmoker.

Therefore, I would suggest you choose two to four months, five months maximum. The exact deadline is up to you. Now, remember, as with your previous decision to be a free, happy nonsmoker, there will be no turning back. When you make the decision, it means that you discard all other possibilities. So, think carefully before actually deciding on your deadline. OK, have you chosen your deadline? Good. Now, stand in front of the mirror. Give yourself a big smile! Yeah, smile to yourself; you are the nicest person in the world, so why shouldn't you smile at yourself?

Last week, I went to London to attend a seminar on leadership. You know what the red line through the entire seminar was?

Yes, *smile!*

People don't smile enough. There is so much power in a big smile! Now, close your eyes and recall that wonderful image of being a free, happy nonsmoker. See the way you look, feel the energy flowing through your veins, enjoy the newly gained emotions. Feel how confident you are. Try to see this image as vividly as possible. Can you communicate with it? Try to say something.

OK, now, with the fresh visualization and emotions of a free, happy nonsmoker in front of you, make your powerful unconditional decision. "I, ..., will be a free, happy nonsmoker by.........!!" Yes! Repeat it! Again! Say it again! Say it out loud! Louder! Shout it all over the place. "I, ..., *will be a free, happy, non-smoker by ....!!"* Great!

Congratulate yourself for making this decision. How does it feel? Do you feel butterflies in your stomach? Yes? It's the positive energy that flows through your body after you have made such a tremendous decision about your Final Liberation and freedom. You have decided that you'll be a free, happy nonsmoker by your specified deadline.

All there is left for you to accomplish is to make sure that your Final Liberation will be a smooth one, without suffering, without withdrawal pains and frustration. Although you have already done a lot towards achieving this. Let's go and have a look at how you can set yourself free without suffering for a split second.

15. Three questions

As we discussed earlier, we have to concentrate on creating new autosuggestions which will help us change our beliefs, fears, and illusions about smoking. By making the decision to become a free, happy nonsmoker by a certain date, you made your first, very powerful step. Automatically your mind will start looking for ways, opportunities, and tools that can help you achieve this goal. The only thing that you should do now is help your mind to get these results faster.

If we analyze our mind and the way it works, we can conclude that our mind is always asking questions. It's through asking questions that we make evaluations: "Do I like this?" "Why do I like that?" Our complete thinking process is based on the questions we ask and the answers we give to these questions. If you agree or disagree with this statement, it actually means that you asked yourself the question, "Do I agree with what I read or not?"

If you want to change the focus of your mind, all you have to do is ask other questions so that your mind can concentrate on something else. If you want to change the ideas you have about smoking, you'll have to develop a new set of questions to ask yourself. This will help you change your focus very quickly. You have to pay attention to the kind of questions you ask.

There is a difference in questions.

The better the questions you ask, the better the answers you can expect. Don't underestimate the power of questions. As we have seen, your subconscious mind always gives back what it is. Therefore, if you ask a poor question, you'll get a poor answer in return.

If you ask, "Why can't I stop smoking?" your mind will do everything to give you an answer. And you'll get an answer, even if your mind invents it. The answers you'll receive may sound like, "Because I've no willpower" or "Because I smoke too much" or "Because I'm an addict." Questions like this will lead you nowhere and will only strengthen your focus on the fact that you can't stop smoking.

It's the kind of questions you ask that determine what you focus on, how you think about things, what your beliefs and convictions are, how you feel, and, finally, what you do. A more powerful question, and certainly a better one, would be, "How can I stop smoking?" This question would immediately shift your focus from one situation where you could never find a possible solution to another one filled with an enormous range of possibilities that would raise new questions leading to more possible solutions. Your mind will finally give you whatever you ask for. Therefore, you have to be careful what you ask for, because you'll always get the answer.

Questions won't only immediately change your focus but by doing so, they will also change the way you feel. If you go back to the first question we have just asked, you'll feel powerless, not inspired, frustrated, irritated, etc. The answer to the second question will give you the feeling of hope, support and empowerment. Further questions will open doors that have so far remained closed. By asking questions, you start to discover new ways you never thought of or ways you blocked out because of previously asked poor questions.

If you ask, "Why do these pills only help in 20 percent of cases?" then you don't consider anything else. You think about pills and you focus on the fact that these pills don't work except for that 20 percent of cases. If you ask, "What else, besides those pills, can I use to help myself?" you are opening your mind to a wide range of ideas and possibilities.

No matter where and how you ask them, questions shape the perception you have about yourself, about others, about what you are capable of, what you believe you can achieve. All the beliefs, illusions, and fears you have regarding smoking have been created by questions and answers to these questions.

These questions and answers have been strongly influenced by heterosuggestions from society, the media, publicity agencies, friends, relatives, etc. These suggestions had years to work on your mind. Their influence came very slowly and softly. Therefore, you hardly noticed that they were further influencing the type of questions you were asking yourself and, consequently, the answers you were receiving.

Just to remind you, a quick example from the past: smoking and stress. When you were stressed, you would light a cigarette to help you cope with the stress. The real reason why you lit a cigarette was the question that you asked yourself, "What can help me reduce my stress at this moment?" Because of heterosuggestions and the internal suggestions from the balloon effect, you came up with the answer that a cigarette is the best tool to help you reduce your stress at that moment.

Therefore, you lit a cigarette. After a while, you don't consciously ask these questions; the result happens automatically, without you even having to think about it. This has a logical explanation. Without going into too much detail of a biological or psychological nature, certain neurons in your brain formed a link. They were connected. The more often you exercise a certain behavior, the more connected these neurons become.

How can you change a behavior, or how can you destroy these bridges between neurons? You do everything either to gain pleasure or to avoid pain. You know that it does not have to be the real pleasure or the real pain that will drive you to do things. If you believe that taking or not taking a certain action will cause you either massive pain or will bring you enormous pleasure, you'll act accordingly. In most cases, we tend to be driven mostly by the fear of a short-term pain rather than the prospect of a long-term pleasure. Procrastination is a very good example of this.

So, pain or pleasure is a very effective way to destroy your behavior or destroy the bridges between the neurons. It's logical that you should link massive pain or enormous pleasure in order to succeed. If you are this far in the book, you should have created a very vivid picture of yourself as a free, happy nonsmoker; a picture where you can see, feel, and experience the way you'll be as a happy nonsmoker. This is your pleasure goal. It's your moment of Final Liberation.

Now you have to associate massive pain with your current situation, namely, with your existence as an imprisoned smoker. One way we have done this throughout the book, without stressing it too much so as to avoid an opposite reaction, is by letting you realize and then admit that you are a drug addict. Certainly subconsciously, this must have caused serious pain to your mind, especially if you have never thought of yourself in this way. You may expect us to start summing up all the bad things we know about smoking; however, nothing is further from the truth. You know what is bad about smoking. You can read. You follow the news. Therefore, there is nothing new to learn about it.

Furthermore, a number of studies have shown that such negative anti-smoking campaigns have little or no effect. The smoker will only strengthen his reasoning for smoking by denying, attacking, or ridiculing the facts presented to him. Let's not forget that your purpose is to remove the desire for cigarettes and nicotine. Once you have achieved this, you won't care what is said about cigarettes and nicotine. Since you have no more need and desire for it, you won't care about it anymore.

We discussed earlier that all our beliefs, fears, and illusions are formed by questions and answers to those questions. What you are going to learn soon is simply to ask yourself a few questions. You are going to do this in a structured and disciplined way; that is, at a certain time and at certain moments. By asking the right questions, you'll be able to destabilize certain fears and illusions you now have about smoking.

Once you've removed these fears and illusions, your need and desire for cigarettes will be over, and you'll be able to consider yourself as a free, happy nonsmoker!! Does this sound too simple to be true? Does this sound too good to be true? Well, this is the only missing step on your journey to Final Liberation. You have already achieved a lot. In the coming days and weeks, you'll construct the grounds for your Final Liberation.

You are not going to ask yourself just any kinds of questions. The questions you are going to ask have to serve your purpose. I have chosen three special questions for you. We will discuss them in a minute. Another issue is when to ask these three questions. This is quite simple: every time you light a cigarette and/or when you extinguish a cigarette.

Let me explain.

Every time you light a cigarette, you ask yourself the three questions, and you answer them for yourself. If you forget to ask the questions when you light your cigarette, you ask them when you extinguish it. The best method would be to ask the questions when you light your cigarette and when you extinguish it.

Let me add something here. Don't panic if you forget once. You'll probably forget quite often. That's fine; I mean, it's not a catastrophe. I strongly advise you to start keeping a daily journal if you haven't done it yet. This is a very good way to evaluate your day. You can write down ideas and reflections you gathered throughout the day.

This is not only a good habit for the coming period to guide to your Final Liberation, but it's a good habit overall. It's a powerful and interesting tool that will help you in several fields. You can use any type of notebook as your journal, or you can order your personal "Success Journal to Final Liberation."

The idea behind the latter is simple. The journey that you are making now is one of the most exciting, not to say the most marvelous, journeys in your entire life. We believe that this journey is worth recording. Afterwards, you'll appreciate that you can relive this exciting journey with all the details you have recorded. If you bought or received the "Full Package to Final Liberation," you have probably already started your success journal.

If so, congratulations!

Don't forget to look back from time to time. You'll be amazed what inspiration you can get out of your own ideas recorded a couple of days ago.

Now let us go back to the questions. You know when to ask them; now you just need to know which questions you need to ask yourself. You know that if you ask bad questions, you'll get bad answers. The simplicity of the questions may surprise you, and that's fine.

The purpose is to keep the questions as easy as possible in order to keep you motivated to ask them as often as possible. Here they are:

1) Why am I smoking this cigarette now?

2) What benefit do I get from this cigarette or what does it give me?

3) Who is the master of the situation, my cigarette or me?

Not too difficult, is it? Let us now review the questions in detail so that I can give you some more explanation about them.

Why am I smoking this cigarette now?

I'm not going to tell you what kind of answers should give; that is something I'll leave up to you. You are the master of your mind. What I want to do here is go over some possible thoughts you might develop and, more importantly, some deeper questions that will arise from asking this basic question. When you first ask yourself the question of why you lit that cigarette, you'll get all kinds of answers; for example, "I just like to light one up," or "I absolutely needed a cigarette!" and so on. Answers like these are fine. You won't notice that after asking this question several times, you always get the same answer. This final answer might surprise you at first. However, once you have found the true answer to the question, you'll realize that you already knew what the answer was. At that moment, it's important to let your mind go further by asking some deeper questions.

What benefit do I get from this cigarette or what does it give me?

At first sight, you might say that this question is the same as the previous one. It's not. What is possible is that your answer to this question is the same as your answer to the first question. This is possible, and this will probably happen in the beginning. That is OK. However, when you think a little bit more about the question, you should be able to come up with better answers. Try to find out what you really get out of the situation. What is the real benefit you created? Is it a short-term or a long-term benefit? What will you achieve from this in the long run? What will you miss in the long term? What benefit will you get from continuing with this? Or what will you gain in the long term? These are the kind of subquestions you'll start asking and answering after a while. I could already give you a list of very powerful subquestions you'll come up with, but this would only spoil the fun and the effectiveness of your thinking process.

The most important thing is that you remember to let your mind go when you notice that it starts asking deeper and more powerful questions. As you can see, it's by asking quality questions that you'll get quality answers. The questions you ask and the answers you give will determine the duration and success of your journey to your Final Liberation.

Who is the master of the situation, my cigarette or me?

This question will make you wonder a bit in the beginning. I believe that by now you have already become quite critical of the current situation you are in. When you light a cigarette, who is really in control? Is it you or is it a cigarette? Do you want a cigarette or does the cigarette want you? It may sound funny at first.

However, when you think back to the balloon effect, it makes more sense, doesn't it? It's important that you ask this question very consciously. Again, it's normal that you'll answer it in a typical way at the beginning. The further you let your mind develop and grow, the better your answers and your analysis will become.

Three questions, hundreds and thousands of answers. That is the beautiful thing about these questions. As you continue your journey, you won't notice how your answers shift from one radical angle to another and then shift once again to an even more radical answer. These questions are the basis for deeper and more powerful questions that will be created with the help and power of your subconscious mind. You might need some discipline at the beginning to ask and answer these questions on a regular basis. Seeing the evolution of your answers will be of great help in progressing on your journey. That is why I told you that it's a good idea to keep a journal.

16. Withdrawal symptoms and pains

What are withdrawal symptoms? Well, I'll tell you what I thought they were and you can see if it corresponds with your story. When I was smoking my four, five packs a day, I wondered what would happen to my body if I quit just like that. I assumed that my body was completely adapted to the fact that it needed a certain amount of nicotine every day and therefore I would only be able to quit by gradually reducing the number of cigarettes smoked each day. I thought that by doing it slowly, my body wouldn't notice it. I considered my body to be a separate entity from myself. I would know it, but my body wouldn't.

If my body were to find out, it would be a catastrophe. It would immediately start suffering, and the pain would be unbearable. Just thinking about not having cigarettes gave me a very nasty panic attack that made me feel miserable. Awful thoughts! I was convinced that I needed medical guidance in order to quit. I thought it would be too dangerous to quit just like that. Even my friends told me that, in my case, as a very heavy chain smoker, it would be advisable to go and see a doctor for advice.

I never went to see a doctor because I couldn't survive the withdrawal symptoms. The pain would be too much to endure. It would be unbearable. You can see now what brainwashing did to me. When I regained consciousness after a five-hour surgery on my neck seven years ago, I fully experienced the power that brainwashing had over me. At that moment I didn't really realize it, but now I see how frightening it is to have your body and your behavior controlled by something else.

They brought me back to my room after surgery; I still was dizzy and not fully awake. Since I'm a heavy sleeper, I generally wake up a little slower. It was a long surgery, and they had given me enough anesthetic to keep me "quiet" throughout the entire surgery. I remember that my parents were in my room. They were very happy that the surgery had gone well. I could hear them whispering. It was a very delicate surgery, and there was some risk that I would come out of it paralyzed. That didn't happen, thank God!

I told the anesthetist before surgery that I wouldn't wake up if I felt any pain and/or if I were paralyzed. I told her that I applied self-hypnosis to program my mind with this suggestion. In a "farewell letter" to my parents, I told them that having to live with a paralyzed son would be hell for them. Therefore, I wouldn't wake up if everything wasn't fine.

When I came round a little bit, I said, "Planner, planner." Quite a strange demand coming from a person still half asleep and recovering. My father thought I just wanted to touch my day planner, to feel something I was familiar with. They put the day planner on my stomach so I could touch it. Then I said, "Letter open, letter open." They understood there was a letter in my day planner. My father took the envelope and, together with my mother, they read my "farewell letter," in which I stated how much I loved them and how grateful I was for everything they had ever done for me.

I could hear both of them crying, and I could see the tears rolling down their cheeks. Then I fell into a deep sleep.

The next time I came around, I tried to move my feet and my fingers. When I felt them move, I was so relieved. I was so happy that everything went fine. I could vaguely see the silhouettes of my mother and sister at the end of the bed. By the light in the room, I determined that it was already evening. I was able to open my eyes a little bit more, but everything remained blurred, and immediately I felt dizzy and very exhausted. Then I said to my mother that I wanted a cigarette...

I couldn't even see or think clearly. I couldn't make the slightest move. I hardly realized that I was awake, and still I was asking for a cigarette. You see how addicted I was! My mother told me I couldn't smoke. It would be too dangerous. I then "ordered" her to ask a nurse for permission, which she did.

However, she came back with the message that it was forbidden. Hearing that, I became furious and told her, in that case, she could leave. I wouldn't see anybody anymore. I had had enough of all this nonsense. So, my mother and sister left. I guess it took only a couple of minutes before I fell asleep again.

The next time I woke up, I was fully awake. I was lying in my bed with a huge brace around my neck, so I couldn't turn my head. I saw some Baxter bags in front of me. One was empty, so I decided to call a nurse. When she came in, I asked her what the bag was for. She asked if I felt any pain. I didn't but I said I did because I was afraid that soon I would.

Then I got the genius idea of how I could smoke a cigarette. If the nurse helped me get out of bed, I could reach for my cigarettes; then I could smoke a cigarette out the window once she was gone. I told her I had to go to the bathroom. She told me that it would be too dangerous and too difficult at the moment. She proposed "the pan." I refused because it didn't fit with my plan. She left surprised, and I was alone in my room.

The only thing I could focus on was obtaining a cigarette as quickly as possible. Was I suffering from withdrawal symptoms? Not at all. OK, let's say it was now about twenty-four hours since I had smoked my last cigarette. I didn't miss anything. It was just the thought of knowing where my cigarettes were and not being able to reach them. I couldn't even sit up by myself. That feeling disturbed me the most. I felt completely dependent on others.

After a while I decided to take control. I tried to push myself up in the bed but that proved impossible. I didn't have a lot of strength left in my arms, and I just couldn't make the move. Then I remembered what the nurse told me before the surgery. She told me that after the surgery, if I wanted to get up, I should turn to my right side, then very slowly shift my legs out of the bed, and then lower them down. Then I had to push myself up, pushing with my left arm crossed over my body.

After a number of attempts and with a bad pain in my neck, I was finally sitting up in my bed, my feet hanging out. I could now reach for my cigarettes lying on the bedside table to my right. I only had to get up a little and then I would have my friends. So I lifted myself up, reached for the table and immediately sat back down! I discovered several small tubes attached to my body; they ran down from my neck, under the sheets, and ended in a transparent basin of blood. I panicked and pushed on the emergency button, wondering what went wrong during the surgery. In the meantime, I discovered another tube and a second blood basin. The nurse came in and I explained to her what I had just discovered.

She calmed me down and explained that everything was fine. It was a standard procedure for cleaning the wound. I was relieved. The nurse asked if she needed to help me get back to bed but I replied that I wanted to sit for a while. She told me to call her if I needed any help and left.

I was now exactly 1.5 meters away from my cigarettes. With some effort I stood up. Finally, I got my cigarettes and I sat down on the bed again. I didn't think about why I needed my cigarettes so badly, I just did it. I was still feeling very tired after the surgery. I was not sure if I actually wanted a cigarette. I suppose it was more the idea of being able to smoke than anything else. Do you know that feeling when you are told you aren't allowed to smoke? Well, it must have been just that.

The next step was to get out of my room and into the smokers' corner. It took quite a bit of effort to reach the smokers' corner. I had to prop myself up against the wall while walking because I could hardly stand on my right leg, as they had taken a piece of bone from it during my surgery. I sat in the corner with the television switched on and finally lit a cigarette. I say "finally," but I didn't feel an urgent need. It felt more like an accomplishment after the surgery.

At around 8:30 a.m., I saw my doctor passing by the smoking corner and heading straight for my room. After a few minutes, he returned and found me in the smokers' corner. He said, "It's always the same; smokers are the first ones to get out of bed! How are you feeling? Pretty good, I guess, if you can make such a trip on your first day." He smiled and left. The remark he made about smokers made me wonder. If you focus your mind on something, you can easily achieve it, as long as you want it badly enough.

You may wonder why I have shared this story with you in this chapter. I could have told it when we spoke about brainwashing. The point is that withdrawal symptoms, about which so many stories exist, were not present in my case. I agree these were special circumstances, and I was probably not in full control of all my senses. The fact that I wanted a cigarette so badly had nothing to do with withdrawal symptoms.

When I look back at it now, I'm still not quite sure what made me crave that cigarette so much. My best guess would be the feeling of being dependent on others, the feeling of powerlessness. It's not so much the cigarette I wanted back, but the feeling of being able to smoke whenever I wanted to. Due to the circumstances I was in, that was impossible. That was the feeling that triggered me off.

The nicotine balloon was also doing its part of the work. It was empty and needed to be filled up. How does it feel? The same as in the situation when you are just about to light a cigarette after not smoking for a while. The hungry, empty feeling. The feeling you have to scratch something, the butterflies. You can describe it in many ways.

But there is one thing it's not: it's not a pain! It doesn't hurt, and it doesn't make you ill! It's very important to realize this. Withdrawal symptoms are hardly noticeable! In fact, you feel these famous withdrawal pains every time you extinguish a cigarette. Have you ever run to the doctor because it hurt too much? Withdrawal symptoms or pains only exist in your head. Not in your body.

When I finally stop smoking, seven years after the surgery, I knew in advance that I wouldn't feel a thing. I wouldn't suffer from a shaking body; I wouldn't be completely overstressed and wouldn't get irritated with everybody and everything. I knew I would be more relaxed and feel great. And that's exactly what happened.

Can you imagine that I, the heavy chain smoker of one hundred cigarettes a day, didn't suffer for a split second when I quit? I can. And you'll be able to. Very soon. The illusion of withdrawal symptoms is another product of the brainwashing around us, sponsored by the pharmaceutical industry, helped by doctors and pharmacists. That's it.

They have created these withdrawal pains in your head. Physically you'll feel absolutely nothing; there is absolutely nothing that will hurt you. You won't feel any pain at all. Your body won't start to shake, and your breathing will be fine—in fact, a lot better than before.

Accept it once and for all: *withdrawal symptoms or withdrawal pains don't exist!* I challenge any doctor or pharmaceutical company to prove me wrong! The only thing that does exist, caused by brainwashing, is the internal withdrawal crisis. This is a mental crisis that occurs in your mind, and these reflections make you believe that there is something wrong with you physically, which isn't the case. If necessary, review chapter two about what you are afraid of.

ॐ

17. Who is in control?

You are the leader of your life, and you control what will happen in it. Every step you take, every decision you make, will have an influence on your future life. While smoking, I wondered from time to time who was in control of my life: my cigarettes or me. Was I the one who determined what I really wanted to do, or were my cigarettes dictating what I did and when I did it? Was I really in control, was I my own boss, or was I just fooling myself into believing this idea? Have you ever asked this question?

Ask yourself right now! Who is the boss in your life? Are you really in charge?

I know the answer, but it may take you a while to find it out. However, the moment will come when you'll find the answer. For now, just think about it from time to time. Especially when you have smoked one of those cigarettes you didn't notice you were smoking. Or when you're standing outside in the cold because you can't smoke inside the building. Or when you are at a reception, anxious to go out to smoke a cigarette, waiting impatiently for the speech to be over so that you can sneak out.

In those moments, ask yourself the question, who is the boss? Who is influencing your behavior on a daily basis? Who is telling you what to do, when to do it, and maybe even with whom?

The moment you find the answer, you'll have to make a choice, either to accept this situation or not. Do I allow something else to control my life? Do I accept being a slave to a cigarette? Do I want to take control of my life again? We all agree that society has reached such a high level of development that we should no longer accept such bad situations and should do everything in our power to ban this kind of abuse.

When it comes to cigarettes, most people have never asked themselves whether it's a legitimate situation and if it's working for them. I didn't at least; have you? In the twenty-five years I smoked, I didn't ask myself why I had accepted being a slave. Why did I accept being a slave of the powerful master called Nicotine? Since I didn't ask the question, I didn't have to think about it, and it was not difficult to accept my situation as, in my eyes, there was no problem. I was a free person, living the way I wanted and enjoying my cigarettes the way I liked. It was just a normal situation, and I didn't feel the need to wonder whether I was a slave or not.

Would I have accepted this situation if I had known I was a slave? Would I have lived voluntarily like a slave for twenty-five years if I had realized what kind of situation I was in? What would you have done? How would you feel if you realized it after twenty-five years? The point of the matter remains that you don't feel like a slave. You know and you admit that you are addicted to cigarettes and maybe you also admit that you are addicted to nicotine, but that's it! You don't think about it much, do you?

Publicity campaigns with cowboys, adventurous men, and extreme sports create the image that smoking is cool. Every time you light a cigarette they want you to feel like a cowboy in the Wild West or like a Range Rover driver in a Camel Trophy. As a girl, you feel like you are losing weight and becoming more attractive. You feel free. The cigarettes provide you with the food that you want, filling the so-called emptiness inside you.

This is the reason why we don't feel like slaves when we smoke. We imagine that we are cool because unconsciously we think back to all the commercials of our favorite brand. We feel great, and we feel that our friend, the cigarette, stops our hunger. Under such conditions, it's rather difficult to feel like a slave. You don't feel mistreated, do you? I remember the time when I was on vacation in Spain.

My parents had a small house outside a nice harbor town. The area was in early development, which meant that apart from our house, there were hardly any other houses there. Since I wasn't allowed to smoke at home, I would go for a walk through the dry and endless prairie that was in front of the house.

About a mile away, there was an old windmill. The building had been destroyed by a storm, and the burning sun had taken its toll. Accompanied by a street dog, I walked around the mill, sat down on a fallen wall, and looked at the horizon. In the background I could hear crickets cooling themselves. I saw the waves of hot air rising from the sand, and then I lit a cigarette. I took my cigarette pack; I grabbed my Zippo from my left back pocket in my jeans, and…click, click. I took the first deep puff, filling my lungs with smoke, and then blew it out slowly, slightly up in the air.

Can you imagine how I felt in that moment? Can you imagine how a fourteen-year-old felt back then? Right, I felt like the almighty cowboy who ruled the entire region and was taking a tour with his loyal dog at his side. What a great feeling! What great publicity! What a great fantasy!

OK, I hear you say, such things can happen to people when they are young and still easily influenced by the publicity they see on TV. You aren't influenced anymore since you are a grown-up. It's true that such image building more easily influences younger people than adults. However, adults are influenced as well. Can't you imagine a situation when you lit a cigarette and felt exactly the same as one of your heroes in your favorite movie? Or going to a bar, lighting a cigarette just before going in, so you feel the same as the man who is getting all the attention from the sexy girls at the bar?

No matter if we are teenagers or adults, we never feel like slaves because we only link nice, cool, and agreeable feelings to smoking. You feel 100 percent in control since you decide when you light the cigarette, what you want to feel, imagine, etc. We are not slaves, come on, we are kings!!

More than twenty years of unconscious slavery? It's hard to understand that I accepted the situation of being a slave for more than twenty years. For twenty-five long years, I had a master that controlled all the things I did, day and night. Unconsciously, your life becomes dominated by the addiction to nicotine. And you just don't realize it…

It's unbelievable how cigarettes have become a part of all your daily activities: when you are on the phone, when you feel bored, when you are having fun, when you get angry, when you are happy, after dinner, when getting into the car, when getting out of the car, before entering a building, when coming out of a building, when feeling sad, before an exciting moment, before you go to sleep, when you wake up, when seducing a partner, after making love, when waiting for someone or something, when working at your desk, when working in the garden, after a swim, when watching a good movie, when walking through the park, when barbecuing, when typing, when reading, etc.

Almost everything you do becomes, in one way or the other, linked to a cigarette.

The truth of the matter is, in your brain, you create a link. Your brain will make a link between a certain activity and smoking a cigarette. This is called neuroassociation. The more often you repeat that specific activity while smoking a cigarette, the stronger the neuroassociation becomes. Since you allow this to happen with almost all your activities, all of them become associated with smoking a cigarette.

One of the activities where I absolutely "needed" a cigarette was when I got into my car. I would smoke a cigarette on the way to my car. Before getting into my car, I would extinguish the cigarette, no matter how much of it I had smoked. Then, I would start the car and light another cigarette. I would only start driving after lighting the cigarette.

On many occasions, I was already sitting in my car when I realized that I didn't have any cigarettes left. So I would get out of the car, go all the way back to my apartment to get a new pack of cigarettes, return to the car, start the car, light the cigarette, and only then drive off.

What I didn't realize was that the cigarette was determining whether I was going to drive or not. No cigarettes, no car. It became worse if I was sitting in my apartment and I hadn't noticed that I was out of cigarettes. I had to go out to buy some cigarettes. I would walk to my car only to realize that I couldn't light a "car cigarette." So, I would leave the car and walk to the supermarket to buy a new pack of cigarettes. I know this may sound absurd, but that is how much cigarettes controlled my behavior.

If you think about your own situation, I mean think deeply about it, I'm sure you'll also find activities where the cigarette fully controls whether or not you are going to do something.

Another example of situations where the cigarette or the nicotine determines what we do is social occasions. I remember participating in receptions and business meetings for my job. While other people were socializing and networking, I was standing outside, sometimes in very cold temperatures, smoking a cigarette. So, the cigarette was deciding whether I would meet new people.

Maybe meeting a certain nonsmoker would be important for my career and thus the future of my life. The cigarette determined who I could meet and who I couldn't, and thus determined how my life was going to turn out. This happens on many other occasions as well. As a smoker, you participate in some activities, but more importantly, you avoid many others and therefore you may miss out on a lot of opportunities. Does this mean that smokers can't be successful or achieve what they want?

No, there are many people who have become very successful in life and yet smoked. The point I'm making is, for a smoker, the chances of missing something are greater than for a nonsmoker.

There is also the psychological effect that many smokers experience. At some point in their smoking life, they come to realize that they are addicted and that they can't stop smoking. They may have tried a number of times without success. Or maybe they have just thought about it but never really gotten around to doing it because they were too afraid. Deep down they feel that they are not in control. They feel that something else is the boss. Something beyond their control is running their daily activities and life in general. They know and experience it on a regular basis.

What they are not aware of, however, is what is happening to them subconsciously. Subconsciously, they are telling their mind that they are not in control, that they don't control the things that happen in their lives, that they don't decide which way to go. Having several failed attempts to quit will also have an influence at a subconscious level. What they are actually telling themselves is that they can't succeed in general.

Having this thought pattern in your subconscious mind can mean a serious block in getting ahead with things or taking any initiatives. And all this because the cigarette is the boss. It's the cigarette that is in control of the situation.

I remember a time, many years ago, when we went fishing with our student club. It was a perfect day in spring, the sun was shining, and it was neither too cold nor too warm. We went out on the North Sea for the whole day. As good students used to, we took a lot of drinks on board, and off we went. After a couple of minutes, one of our friends realized that he forgot his cigarettes. We told him it was not a problem since the rest of us had more than enough cigarettes to share with him.

Although his first problem was solved, he remained in a bad mood. He said he missed his cigarettes and he couldn't light a cigarette whenever he wanted. Each time he had to ask one of us, which was too much for him. It didn't agree with his smoking pattern.

So he remained in a bad mood for the rest of the day. Even though he could smoke as much as he liked, his mood didn't improve because he didn't have his own cigarettes with him. The cigarettes took control of how he felt that day.

After a great day of fishing and having fun, we returned to the port in Ostend. When we left the boat, our friend immediately ran to his car, opened the door, and grabbed his own pack of cigarettes and a lighter. He felt as if he was born again! In the evening, when we went to the casino, our friend was in a completely different mood.

Even though he was losing at roulette, he felt great and was pleased with the whole day. All that changed because he got his cigarettes back. He completely forgot that he was a real pain in the neck all day long. He forgot that he didn't enjoy himself, compared with the rest of the group.

That's how strongly a cigarette can occupy your mind. You don't see reality as it is. You look at everything through your nicotine glasses. How can it be that you don't actually notice these things are happening? Why do you allow the cigarette to control your daily life, and why aren't you really aware of it?

As we read in the chapter about the balloon effect, the feelings we become aware of are so insignificant, meaningless, that we don't really pay attention to them. It feels like being a little hungry; that's it. Nobody suspects that this feeling is going to determine what one does or doesn't do during a day. We certainly don't think that it can influence our social activities because we consider it our partner, our friend that accompanies us everywhere we go. We even have the illusion that the cigarette helps us make the event better or more intense.

When I discovered who was actually running my life, I tried to deny it. I can tell you, it's not a nice feeling to find out that for the past twenty-five years, something else was in control of my life. Knowing that this something else was a cigarette didn't make me feel any better. I guess that some of you are still protesting against the idea that a cigarette controls your life. It's true that you could use it as an excuse for many things that happened or didn't happen in your life. That is, of course, not the intention. What I want you to realize is that cigarettes have a greater impact on you than you could ever imagine.

How many car accidents have been caused by a cigarette? How many lives have been lost? How many lives have been completely changed as a result? I could go on and give thousands and thousands of examples to make it very clear that cigarettes dominate your life in one way or the other.

What if you only smoke five cigarettes a day? People who smoke a few a day think that they are in full control of the situation. They actually don't think they are addicted. Therefore, they usually don't quit easily. They believe that they control the situation because they decide when they smoke. Some of them smoke only after 5:00 p.m. Others smoke exactly one cigarette after each meal, one before going to bed and one when waking up. Others call themselves "occasional smokers," and they only smoke when they are at a reception, a party, or in company.

If they think they control the situation, they are wrong. If they really controlled the situation, why would they still be smoking? If they think they smoke because they like it, then why don't they smoke all day long?

Is it not because, deep down, they know it's not good for their health? They know it would be better not to smoke, and that's why they try to control themselves during the day. These people actually suffer constantly. Not because of withdrawal symptoms, no, but because they deprive themselves of something they really want: their cigarette, their partner in difficulties. Every single day they fight as well as they can against nicotine addiction. Every day they lose several times.

The balloon effect is always present, and they must have nerves of steel to survive all day. They tell themselves that it was a good day since they smoked so few cigarettes. The cigarette is in full control of what you do, when you do it and how you do it. The cigarette determines how you feel during the day, how long you feel this way, and what you have to do to change the state you are in.

The fact that you smoke at a certain time of the day or the fact that you smoke five cigarettes says nothing except that you have strong willpower to resist. In addition, these people are conditioning themselves for the brainwashing they already got from society. They have the idea that they are missing something.

This will also play an important role when you consider quitting. On the one hand, you don't feel like quitting because you believe that everything is fully under control. On the other hand, deep down you know very well how much you would suffer after quitting. If you were to quit completely, it would only become worse and worse.

Moreover, smoking like this gives smokers the illusion that smoking is actually good. When they finally smoke a cigarette, the balloon is completely empty, and they get the impression that the cigarette tastes really good and gives them such a great feeling. The real reason for their well-being is the fact that the balloon is inflated again.

I am moving away from what I wanted to tell you. I discovered that the cigarette was the boss dictating my life. Everything I did, in one way or another, was related to smoking! I started looking for things I did where the cigarette wouldn't play a role.

Taking a shower or a bath, no, I would shower quicker when I was without cigarettes, and I would stay longer in my bath when I had my cigarettes so I could smoke in the bath. Sleeping? No, I would wake up to smoke, and when I was younger I would stay up longer in order to smoke a cigarette out the window.

Reading? No, I would sit next to an ashtray so I wouldn't have to get up every time I wanted a cigarette. Traveling, eating, drinking, talking, laughing, writing, working, doing sports, all these things were heavily influenced and controlled by the cigarette. I was filled with indignation. How could a cigarette dominate me and my life?

Freedom stands very high on my value scale so to discover that I was not a free human being, that my life was run by a cigarette was a very disturbing and difficult concept. It was even more difficult to accept. I ran around with this idea for a couple of weeks, focusing on every situation, analyzing who was in control, who was the boss?

How about you? How do you feel about it at this moment? Some of you are already convinced that you are dominated by the cigarette. Others will still have to go through this stage. Don't worry about it now, that's for later. But it's good if you have already spent some time considering who the boss is.

Once I accepted it, I knew it had to change. I knew that I had to become the master of my life again. At the same time, I was very scared, because by accepting the fact that the cigarette was my boss, the idea of quitting smoking forever seemed to move further and further away. How would I ever be able to stop smoking if cigarettes influenced everything I did? Could I change knowing that nicotine had dominated my life for more than twenty-five years? Although I didn't know the answer, I felt I was on the right track. I realized the truth of my situation.

I knew where to start. I was convinced of one thing; I would regain control over my life. I would no longer tolerate something else dominating me in such a drastic way—drastic in the sense that it went almost unnoticed. I became a slave without even being aware of it. I hear you say that if it happened unnoticed, why bother? Well, if you aren't bothered, why are you reading this book? It does matter. Everyone has the right to be a free person, truly free from any addiction that is controlling his or her life. And you'll become free in a short while!

‿

18. Your personal success journal to your Final Liberation

Having support on your journey to Final Liberation will help you achieve your goal in a faster and easier way. A journal can provide such a support, and you'll experience it as a mental follow-up on your way to success.

Every day, concentrate for five minutes on your smoking behavior by writing down which cigarette you enjoyed the most. Was it the cigarette in the morning when you were still lying in bed? That was my favorite one, or should I say those were my favorite ones, as I would usually smoke three or four cigarettes before even getting out of my bed.

Maybe your favorite cigarette is the one you smoke at the breakfast table with your first cup of coffee. Is it the cigarette you smoke in your car, when you're all by yourself and enjoying some good morning music?

What were the answers to my three questions today? Was there anything special about today? What do you think about your thinking pattern? Is it still the same as yesterday? What evolution have you made since the beginning? Using a journal will be very helpful in analyzing your behavior and finding out why you do certain things. It will give you an insight into your daily patterns of smoking.

You'll be surprised how the daily routine of writing in your personal journal puts your subconscious mind to work. It will be there all the time, working for you in the background, analyzing the situation, looking for answers, searching for solutions. You should see your journal as your soul mate who accompanies you on the great journey you are undertaking.

As with many other things, it's much easier to do or achieve something when you are with someone else, isn't it? Well, this is how you should see your journal. Share it, praise it, and give it all the necessary time and respect it deserves. Eventually you will treat yourself with a lot more respect and give yourself all the care you need.

When you write in your journal on a daily basis, you won't notice that it becomes a good friend. Your journal is a place where you can release all your thoughts and all the feelings and frustrations you have about smoking. The process of writing down these thoughts will be a kind of healing therapy. You'll feel relieved, and your mind will be strengthened for the new challenges on your path to Final Liberation.

As your journey is a very exciting one, it's always nice to have something to record it in. The journey you are about to undertake will be one of the most exciting journeys you'll ever make in your entire life. Wouldn't it be good if, after a while, you could read about your progress? Wouldn't it be interesting to see how your thought patterns evolved from day to day? Wouldn't you feel proud while reading about the different steps you took along the road?

The best way to use your journal is on a daily basis. If, for some reason, you are not able to write in it for a day, that's fine. However, try not to forget too often. It's, as I said earlier, a true friend and support on your journey to your Final Liberation.

Maybe you could choose a certain time during the day to write in your journal. For some of you the best time would be in the morning, while for others it will be at night, just before going to bed. I mostly write just before going to bed. This helps me to gather my thoughts and review the day as a whole.

The most important thing is that you do it. Make a habit of it. Five minutes will do. Gradually you'll realize how powerful it is, and the inspiration it can give you.

You don't have to write every day in the same way that you don't have to do any of the things I mention in the book. I'm just sharing some thoughts with you because I believe they will be helpful on your journey to becoming a free, happy nonsmoker.

The question you should ask yourself whenever you think you don't have time is, "How much time do I have for myself every day?" It is very important to ask this question in our busy lives. We don't make time for ourselves anymore. All we do is rush to get things done. By the end of the day we have done plenty of things, except finding time for ourselves. We have no time to think about what we made of the day. What were the wonderful things that happened today?

What are the lessons we could learn from today?

While going through such an important change in your life, it's crucial that you give yourself that gift. Spend a couple of minutes a day on yourself and with yourself. Analyze those questions, think about your smoking behavior, and always keep the picture of your decision in front of you: "I'll be a free, happy nonsmoker!"

You can write as long as you want in your journal. Frankly, I advise you to do it all the time, since it gives you so much in return. I once read that if your life is worth living, it's worth recording. I believe this is a real truth. If you reason like this and write in your journal every day, you'll try to make it a special and exciting day which is worthwhile writing about.

As for your journey to Final Liberation, I advise you to continue writing even after you have lived your Final Liberation moment. Share the thoughts of your first days of liberation. Write down how it makes you feel energized, free, exciting. You'll have a lot of fun rereading it years from now. Keep track of your new life in the weeks and months that are ahead.

I would like to receive a copy of your journal, especially the part that describes what happened in your life from the day you became a free, happy nonsmoker. Share your thoughts and experiences with the world and send us a copy. With your permission, it will be published with your name as part of my next book. You'll find more explanation in an upcoming chapter.

❧

19. My last cigarette

You and I have had a nice journey so far. Let me congratulate you on the fact that you are still here with me. Unfortunately, many others have left us during the process. Not because quitting smoking is so hard, but because reading this book is so hard! But you kept on reading and working on yourself, which is great. And the best part is still to come. You'll be greatly rewarded for your efforts; you'll become a free, happy, energetic, and enthusiastic nonsmoker. How does that feel?

I remember my last cigarette as if it were yesterday! Why? No, not because it was difficult. It was truly one of the greatest moments in my entire life!!! It was absolutely the best victory party I ever experienced! I felt so unbelievably great, warm, filled with positive vibes; it was just magnificent—even though it happened in a terminal at Frankfurt Airport and I was all by myself.

I flew in from Brussels to Frankfurt, where I had to take a connecting flight to Budapest. This was one of my usual routes I took at that time. Sunday evening, I would fly from Brussels to Frankfurt, wait a while in the Senators' Lounge, and then take a connecting flight to Budapest, where I was working on a project.

That Sunday wasn't any different from every other Sunday, except for one thing. I decided that I would smoke my last cigarette at Frankfurt airport between the two flights I had to take that day. Big decision!

Well, actually it wasn't. As I mentioned, I had already been questioning myself for a couple of months about why I was smoking and how I could quit without suffering for a split second. A few days earlier, I felt absolutely convinced that I had found the way and that I could stop smoking at any moment. I absolutely knew that I could stop smoking just like that and I could do it without suffering.

Choosing the right date wasn't such a hard thing to do. I don't know why I picked that Sunday. Looking back, I'm glad I decided on that Sunday and not one week later, because otherwise I might not have been able to write this book. I didn't know at that moment that I would be in a serious car crash four days later.

Anyway, I chose that Sunday when I came off the plane from Brussels. As usual, the first thing I did after leaving the plane was to light a cigarette. I already found it funny, since I had broken the magical code to my Final Liberation, allowing me to see through all the illusions about nicotine. Nevertheless, I wanted to stick to my rituals for a while.

What I liked about Frankfurt airport were the smoking corners. This was very practical when you had to walk from one terminal to another. Heavy smokers like me could rest every five hundred meters and smoke a cigarette. I always found this quite amazing, because in most airports smoking is prohibited. The thing you find are dirty smoking rooms packed with smokers from the entire airport, breathing in each other's smoke. You don't even need to light a cigarette in these rooms, just breath normally and you'll get a double dose. The worst one I ever visited was the Atlanta airport. Just awful! When I opened the door, a thick wall of smoke hit me. I had to adapt quickly to the conditions in that room; even I found it disgusting.

To continue with my story, I went to the Senators' Lounge, where, as usual, I had a Diet Coke and some crackers. In that lounge there was a big area for smokers. Nonsmokers had tables, chairs, and nice, soft, leather seats. The smokers didn't get that privilege. I sat down at a table and started making some phone calls. It was a part of my traveling ritual, calling friends and family to kill the time between flights. That day I had a special message for my friends: "I'm going to smoke my last cigarette in a couple of minutes!"

Their reactions were quite funny, "Are you kidding? No? Oh, well, good luck. Because if you can stop smoking, I can, too." One friend asked, "How do you feel? Aren't you nervous? No? Well, we'll see. Good luck with it." Another wanted to know if I was serious about quitting or just kidding with them.

I called quite a few people and most of them were rather surprised. They were surprised that I was calling them before I actually quit. It would take me too long to explain to them that, in my mind, I had already quit. The decision was made; the desire for cigarettes was completely gone. I was already a free person!

About twenty minutes before I had to take the other plane, I went to the terminal. That day it was terminal C, which is a small terminal at Frankfurt airport. I walked through a small wing and came across a bar where a few people were having a drink. I went to the bar, ordered a Coke and a ho tdog. And, of course, I lit a cigarette. When I left home, I had taken one precaution. I left my Zippo at home. I took an ordinary lighter with me because I knew I would leave my cigarettes and lighter somewhere in the airport.

There I was, standing at that small bar, eating my hot dog and smoking one of my last cigarettes. Next to me stood an older man, I guess he must have been in his fifties, drinking whiskey and smoking a cigar. I noticed that all the people at the bar were smoking, probably because this was the area where they could smoke.

I could tell from his eyes that it was not his first whiskey that evening. Then I decided to smoke my final cigarette. I opened my pack and took a cigarette. There were about seven cigarettes left in the pack. I lit the cigarette and inhaled deeply.

While I was smoking, I tried to analyze each puff and everything I felt. I imagined the smoke filling my lungs and then my lungs reacting to the smoke. I wanted to feel the effect that the cigarette had on me. I concentrated on the taste it left in my mouth. I was checking whether the whole thinking process I went through in the last two months was working. I knew it would, and now I could experience it vividly.

The cigarette had a dry and disgusting taste, I didn't get any pleasure out of it, and it was doing nothing for me. I took another puff and then closely examined the cigarette. I saw how the white paper was slowly burning. I saw the fire hit a small sulfur ring. I observed how I held the cigarette between my fingers. It made me think about the beginning of my smoking history. My fingers were completely yellow and smelled of nicotine. Over time, although I smoked more, my fingers lost their yellow color. The only way that I could explain it was that my body and fingers got used to the nicotine and adapted.

I was thinking how strange that movement actually was, holding the cigarette between your two fingers and bringing it to your mouth. I thought about how, in the past, that movement had generated feelings of pride, security, trust, control.

I was observing other smokers at the bar. One seemed to be smoking his cigarette without even consciously experiencing what he was doing. You could see that for him, smoking was a constant feeding process for the big balloon inside him. He smoked one cigarette after another, not realizing that he was inhaling deeply every couple of seconds. I looked at the ashtray I was using, and I thought it was the last time I would be so close to an ashtray. I observed the ashes lying in it, covered in stubs from all kinds of brands. The bartender emptied the ashtrays once a day, so I had a good collection in front of me.

While I was staring at the ashtray, I asked myself how it was possible that for more than twenty-five years, I did something that produced such a dirty waste. I took the ashtray to smell it. It was awful! Seeing and smelling this, I wondered how I could ever have convinced myself that a cigarette tasted good.

To check whether I was right, I took another puff from my cigarette. It really didn't taste good. I wondered why I had to do this any longer.

Even though I wanted to extinguish it, I continued to smoke it. I had to smoke it to its very end. I was going to "kill" the cigarette now. Once and for all. I wanted to feel, smell, touch, and taste everything about that cigarette. I wanted to be absolutely sure that there would be nothing at all that I would miss, like, love, or need.

That was the condition I had set for myself: finding a way to stop smoking without suffering for one split second. In my head, the decision was made a long time ago, and the illusions were all gone. I took one or two more puffs and blew the smoke in the air.

That was something I wouldn't be doing anymore. No more smoke through my nose, no more smoke rings in the air, no more smoke blown into my girlfriend's face. Gone. All smoke would be gone, including the black smoke that had been around my mind for so many years. In a few moments, I would be free at last. Free from nicotine, free from the slavery of nicotine. Free from needing a cigarette every five or ten minutes, free from worrying where my cigarettes were or how many cigarettes I still had left. Free from driving to a tobacco store at 2:00 a.m. Free from the black clouds in my head. And free from all the guilt I had for all those years.

Deep down, I always felt guilty about damaging my health. I had carried the feeling of being a loser. How else could I feel? I wanted to stop smoking, but I was always too afraid to give it a try.

All these negative thoughts and feelings would soon be over. Actually, they were already over. I was already free in my mind. I was already a nonsmoker because I no longer had the desire for cigarettes. I couldn't think of any reason to smoke another cigarette. I was finally free! So that was it. I took the last deep puff of my cigarette. I extinguished the cigarette in the ashtray with a kind of victorious move and gave it a final deadly turn, just to be sure that it was really gone. Immediately I had this great, warm, and glorious feeling. I felt so satisfied! I looked with a kind of supremacy at the other people in the bar.

I was *free!*

I was completely free from the worst slavery ever!

From now on, I could go and walk wherever I wanted. I didn't have to pay attention to what I could or I couldn't do. I was in full control of my body. It felt great.

I left the bar and went in the direction of my gate. I left my pack of cigarettes on the bar table. When I was about ten meters away from the bar, I heard the older man shouting to me, "Sir, you forgot your cigarettes!" I felt so proud when I heard it. I turned around and I called back, "You can have them, I just quit!" "But your lighter is in it" answered the old man. "I won't need it anymore!" I said. I turned around and walked victoriously to my gate. I still remember the surprised look on the old man's face. I could see he was happy that he could have my cigarettes but I could feel the pain that went through him because he realized he was still a slave to nicotine.

A few minutes later, the gate opened and we all boarded the plane to Budapest. During the flight I enjoyed my victory. I thought back to the moment at the bar. I thought about all the times I had been afraid to quit. In that moment I felt like I could rule the world. I felt lighter, as if a heavy weight had finally fallen from my shoulders.

The flight took about ninety minutes, but it seemed like a couple of minutes. Everything looked so different. I wanted to shout out loud that I was a free person. I achieved my Final Liberation. I had just set myself free from the biggest slavery of our century.

When I walked through the terminal at Budapest Airport, I thought to myself that I normally would have been smoking a cigarette. I had to laugh at the idea. I could picture myself. Grabbing my pack of cigarettes, lighting a cigarette, looking around to see if there were any police or guards, and then quickly taking a few puffs before going through customs. Once I had passed customs, I would have lit a new cigarette while waiting for my luggage. That could take a while in Budapest, so quite often I would have smoked two cigarettes before getting my suitcase.

But here I was, walking through customs, with a big satisfied smile on my face, heading to the conveyer belt to pick up my luggage. I said to myself, "Eric, a-ha, normally you would have lit a cigarette by now!" I was really enjoying the situation and my great victory. Instead of feeling empty or experiencing withdrawal pains, I felt unbeatable and proud of my Final Liberation and victory.

When I came out of the airport, I said again to myself, "Eric, a-ha, normally you would have lit a cigarette now, a-ha, how silly." I went to the taxi boy and ordered a taxi. Normally I would have lit a cigarette, probably managing two or three puffs. When the taxi arrived, I realized that I *didn't* have to ask if I could smoke in his car, because I didn't need to.

During the trip to the hotel, I wondered why I had smoked all those cigarettes in the past. For what good reason had I ever smoked them? I couldn't find any good reason at all. Not the taste, not the excitement, not the pleasure. The best reason I could find was, "Eric, a-ha, normally you would have lit a cigarette." That was more than enough. I replaced the need for smoking a cigarette with the victorious feeling of regaining control of every single inch of my body and mind. That was the most incredible feeling ever.

The taxi arrived at the Intercontinental Hotel and the bellhop helped me with my luggage. The receptionist greeted me and said that my room was all set. As I was a regular customer there, they knew my preferences, and most of the time they gave me a room with a nice view over the Donnau River and the old romantic bridge.

I knew I had to ask for another room that night. I needed a non-smoking room! So, very proudly I asked the receptionist if he could arrange a *non*smoking room for me. He looked at me and saw me glowing with pride. He said, with real conviction, "Congratulations, sir. Well done!" "Kussenem," I said, which means "thank you" in Hungarian.

I felt so proud, so wonderful that I had received this simple but true recognition. I entered my hotel room and could smell the cold freshness of a clean room. That was a change. I used to enter rooms that smelled of nicotine and smoke. Even as a heavy smoker, I could smell it every time I got into those rooms. Now I had a really fresh room, on a smoking-free floor in the hotel. What a difference!!

To celebrate my Final Liberation, I hurried downstairs to the bar. I sat by the window with a very nice view of the Donnau and the old bridge. Again I thought to myself, "A-ha, normally I would have lit a cigarette!" I truly enjoyed every time I said that to myself, mainly because it made me see so clearly why it was, and is, so unnecessary, where in the past I considered it a necessity. I think I was lighting up in some way, because most people looked at me with a strange expression. I guess they must have felt some of that victorious sensation that I was experiencing.

I stayed in the bar for about half an hour, and then I went to my room to sleep. Normally I would have smoked a couple of cigarettes before switching off the light. Now, I felt relaxed, watched some television, and went to sleep.

※

20. The first nicotine-free day

The next morning I woke up and I enjoyed the fact that my room didn't smell like nicotine and tobacco. I didn't have any desire for a cigarette. I felt much more energized when I came out of the shower. When I was still a smoker, I would have smoked two or three cigarettes by that time. I kept reminding myself by saying, "A-ha, normally I would have." I was replacing the act of smoking a cigarette with joy by internally laughing at my past comic situation.

Eating my breakfast, I was amazed how much better my food tasted. At first I wasn't aware of it, and then it slowly came to me that everything had a different taste. I realized that it was the first result of being a nonsmoker. After breakfast, I took a taxi to the project, and again I thought I would have smoked at least two cigarettes, if I were still smoking.

When I arrived at the office, I immediately communicated the great news to my staff. Because I felt so certain of myself, I told it in a bizarre and funny way: "I just stop smoking yesterday evening, so anyone who is thinking of stressing me today better think it over. You might just end up on the sidewalk!"

Although everybody laughed at my "threatening message," I could see a few worried faces. They were influenced and brainwashed by society. Heterosuggestions had convinced them that someone who quits smoking becomes intolerable, at least for a while. So there I was, sitting in the office, without cigarettes. Some of the staff members who smoked looked at me whenever they lit a cigarette. It didn't bother me. I felt sorry for them and wished they would also find the way to their Final Liberation.

The day went fine, without any extra stress, without any withdrawal pains, no getting nervous, and no shaking body. The only thing I felt was freedom and victory. I felt so confident because after twenty-five years and about one million cigarettes, I had become a free, happy, and joyful nonsmoker. Not one thought about smoking crossed my mind. It was definitely behind me.

I can hear you saying, "How did you know? So many ex-smokers start again, after one month, one year, ten years, etc." That's true. However, as you already know by now, they must have forgotten something. Or rather, they didn't experience something when they quit. They never experienced this huge revelation and liberation of quitting smoking. When they quit, they probably felt lousy. They felt like they were missing out on something. They kept themselves busy until the day when a weak moment arrived, the "missing feeling" became too strong, and they started smoking again.

What I experienced, and what you are about to experience, is quite different. Even before smoking your last cigarette, you'll absolutely know that you don't need another cigarette in your life. You won't only know it, you'll feel it. It fills your entire body. You are at that point a nonsmoker. Period.

Don't forget that a nonsmoker does not have the desire to smoke. A nonsmoker simply does not need a cigarette. The reason why so many nonsmokers become smokers is discussed earlier in this book. They become victims of heterosuggestions from society, brainwashing, and, of course, nicotine addiction. By now you should be able to see through all of them, so there is no risk that you could fall into the trap of these suggestions.

During my first free day, I continued to repeat to myself my now famous phrase, "A-ha, normally I would have smoked a cigarette now, a-ha!" It increased my pleasure. I didn't have the feeling that it was bad to think about cigarettes. This is something I strongly advise you to remember when your moment comes. There is nothing wrong in thinking about your old smoking behavior. In fact, it's good.

When you think of your old smoking behavior, even though you know that it was not the best thing to do, you get affirmation of your right choice. So what you are actually doing is replacing the so-called pleasure you had from smoking a cigarette with the real pleasure of looking back and enjoying the moment of being absolutely free from nicotine slavery.

The staff was completely surprised that I stayed so calm through-out the whole day. They thought, remembering how much I smoked in the past, that I wouldn't be able to control my nerves. It couldn't be further from the truth. Why would I be nervous? Why would I become crazy?

The only thing to be crazy about was the fact that I was finally free!!! I was a free human being and I could start enjoying my life. I had beaten the unbeatable! I achieved what I and many other people con-sidered impossible. It gave me a great feeling of success, achievement, victory, and power. I thought I could rule the whole world. Without any doubt, it was the best feeling I had ever felt in my entire life.

The evening didn't differ much from the day. From time to time, I mentioned to others and myself when I normally would have smoked a cigarette. Most people were astonished. They claimed that I would start smoking again within hours or days. They were all brainwashed by the heterosuggestions of our society. They couldn't imagine that somebody who smoked four packs a day could quit just like that without any effort or suffering.

The reason why I describe the process of "my last cigarette" in so much detail is to make you familiar with the situations and feelings you are going to experience once your moment of Final Liberation has come. This is so you can better visualize this wonderful moment. Imag-ine how you would feel if you knew right now that you would never want to smoke another cigarette! Imagine the feeling of freedom and victory that would go through you. It's all yours.

On that first day after the big event, I went to bed with the strongest and greatest feelings I had ever felt. I was so full of what was happening. I had confidence, I felt glorious, my sense of taste changed enormously, I could smell things much better. Those dark clouds in my mind were gone. It was just fantastic. I was lying in my bed and thinking back on the day. I tried to remember any moment when I'd had difficulties or negative feelings or thoughts, and I couldn't!! Wasn't that amazing? I couldn't recall any negative feeling, signs, or associations with cigarettes.

My mind was completely free of any desire, lust, or feelings towards nicotine and cigarettes. I was a newborn, free person. It was as if cigarettes had never existed in my life. The rest of the week passed in a similar manner.

I didn't experience any of those negative effects the doctors and pharmaceutical companies spoke about. I was in the best of moods, to the surprise of my staff. Their surprise grew with each passing day. They could hardly believe that I was keeping it up for so long. Some started to notice that there was something different happening. They saw that it wasn't just another try. They started to realize that it was a new, permanent state in which I would continue.

Others were betting on the fact that I would eventually give up. That is why they call it "giving up." In their brains, as in the brains of millions of other people, smoking is about giving up. Let me tell you again, there is nothing to give up when you stop smoking. There are only many great things to win!

I arrived at Brussels Airport the following Friday afternoon. It was a milestone in my life. I would set foot on Belgian ground for the first time in twenty-five long years of slavery as a free, nonsmoking person! It felt fantastic! I walked off the plane into the huge new terminal. I had a big smile on my face and said to myself, "A-ha, one week ago I would have lit a cigarette by now! Unbelievable!" Repeating that phrase gave me such pleasure, such a victorious feeling, that I jumped in the air. I would leave this airport as a happy nonsmoker. In a couple of hours I would face Belgium and meet my friends and family as a happy non-smoker!! And there was nothing that could stop me.

That night I was invited to a birthday party of a friend of mine. It would be my first real party since I stop smoking. It would be another great victory. It was a great party! We had a lot of fun, and the people I met respected my "heroic" deed. They had lots to say: "Whoa, I hope you'll hang on." "Good luck! How did you do it?" "Does it hurt? How do you feel after a couple of days?" My friends and people who knew me better doubted me. They said, "You won't hold on very long!" "Do you know how difficult it is to quit?" "What are you doing to yourself? Come on, you know you won't succeed. Quit torturing yourself." Sometimes you need to hear those things from your friends.

One morning, I came up with an idea. I had to tell as many peo-ple as possible how I stopped smoking without suffering! The more I thought about it, the clearer it became. I had to write a book about the way I stopped smoking so that other people could use the same method to quit. I would visit schools and colleges to give speeches about smoking and how to quit.

I would do radio interviews and TV interviews for all the major channels in Europe and the United States. The message couldn't remain just my message. It belonged to everybody. All the people still enslaved by nicotine should know the way to Final Liberation! I would bring out this easy to follow method so that thousands and thousands of people could stop smoking without suffering.

I immediately considered writing the book in English. English is the most universal language, and it would allow me to reach a large num-ber of people. I knew I would be able to help more people if I wrote in English. The book would also be translated into Spanish, French, my mother tongue, Dutch, and many other languages. That was my dream! I would leave my mark on earth by helping people to liberate themselves from the biggest slavery of the twenty-first century, the slavery of nicotine! I started dreaming about all those happy, liberated faces of so many new nonsmokers. I want you to realize that if you are reading these words right now, you are making this dream a reality! And do you know what the best part of it is? It won't only be a huge celebration for me, as my dream becomes reality, but a victory for you, as you will be *free* from nicotine in a very short while.

I know that some of you are already free of nicotine at this very moment. You already know that you can extinguish this cigarette and never ever want another one in your entire life. Take your time, though; there is no need to hurry. Those of you who don't feel this way yet, or at least not completely, please don't worry at all. Just relax and continue reading the book. That's the only way you'll make your dream, our dream, come true.

⁓

21. The Final Liberation

When your Final Liberation comes, you'll know it. You'll just feel it. It's difficult to describe this feeling. It is as if a weight has fallen from your shoulders. By reading the book, by questioning your illusions and fears in a structured way, you have given your subconscious mind all the ideas and information it needs to analyze, process, and change its image of smoking. Step by step, you have changed the references, the experiences, and ideas you had about smoking. Your subconscious mind is now ready to guide you and protect you on your journey to live as a free and happy nonsmoker. It has all the powers necessary to do just that. Relax and enjoy your Final Liberation.

You'll see through all the illusions. You'll ask yourself how you could have been so blind for all these years. You'll see clearly that cigarettes don't have any benefits. Those were just illusions, created by the genius trap called nicotine. You have cleared your mind of all the brainwashing of hetero-suggestions. You feel great, victorious, and powerful simply because you know you have conquered your biggest enemy. You also know that you have conquered it forever; it's dead! It's dead because *you* killed it. You personally witnessed the death of your slavery. You reached your Final Liberation.

You can breathe freely and enjoy the fresh air. You can go wherever you want without needing or craving the cigarettes that have controlled your life for so long. You can decide what you'll do, when, and how. There is nothing that will control you or your actions anymore. No more limits, no boundaries. You are a free, happy non-smoker!! You have liberated yourself from one of the worst slaveries humanity has ever known. To this day, in our civilized world, we are still fighting one of the biggest, most brutal, and most lethal slaveries ever known to mankind.

You have freed yourself from it! Celebrate!

See how you take control of your life again; enjoy the feeling of victory and freedom. Sense these moments of relief. Put yourself in ecstasy! Consider that you have achieved what you thought impossible. Share this moment, anchor it in your mind, as one of the best experiences you'll ever have in your life. You'll feel so great. When you have reached this moment, you know you can proceed to the final ritual; smoking your last cigarette!

Some of you may wonder whether you still have to smoke this last cigarette. If you are in this situation right now, you can surely celebrate! You have achieved what you wanted to achieve. You have no desire for a cigarette. It has become completely clear to you that smoking gives you nothing. You understand that there is absolutely nothing to give up since smoking does nothing for you. The answer whether or not you should smoke this last cigarette is a definite *yes!*

I'll come back to that in a minute. Is there anybody who still has doubts? Do you still feel uncomfortable when you think that you are going to smoke your last cigarette? Do you feel like celebrating, or do you feel a little down and depressed because of what you are going to do? If it's the second, don't worry. There is absolutely nothing to worry about. Just continue for a couple of days or weeks asking and answering questions, reread some chapters of the book. Analyze the thoughts and notes in your journal and let your subconscious mind do the rest. Remember, each night to focus on the picture of your decision to be a free, happy nonsmoker! Live it, feel it, smell it, and enjoy it. Your Final Liberation is coming closer and closer.

Now that you are ready for your last cigarette, there are a few things I would like you to do. You have done a great deal so far, so you'll have no problems fulfilling these last instructions.

First of all, I want you to go back to your decision to be a free, happy nonsmoker. I want you to see this picture very clearly in front of you! You are now ready to act upon this decision. By smoking this next and last cigarette, you accomplish your goal of never, ever smoking another cigarette in your life. The ritual of smoking this final cigarette is a milestone in your journey to Final Liberation.

From now on, you'll think about smoking in the following way: "Yeah, I'm a free, happy nonsmoker! Ha!" There is no other thought possible. Smoking does absolutely nothing for you. Remember that if you could go back to the moment before you smoked your first cigarette, you would do so, and you wouldn't miss a single thing. Well, that's exactly what you are about to do.

While smoking your last cigarette, pay special attention to every single detail of that moment. Look at the shape of the cigarette; observe how the smoke lifts up. Concentrate on the taste when you inhale. What does it smell like? Feel the balloon inflating while you inhale the nicotine. Imagine how the balloon creates this illusion of emptiness. How does your mouth feel? What do you feel in your throat as you blow out the smoke? Yes, have a final look at yourself as a smoking "machine" and see what a "charming" picture it is. Ask yourself how you could have been so stupid for so many years, inhaling that dirty smoke that tastes so awful. Experience it fully!

Now, extinguish your cigarette and celebrate this moment of victory! "Kill" your final cigarette in a ritual way. Feel victorious and free. Feel how freedom is welcoming you. Imagine huge black chains that you have just cut through and pulled off.

Celebrate your moment of freedom. Remember that there is nothing wrong in thinking about smoking. On the contrary, think about the moments that you would have lit a cigarette and then say to yourself, "A-ha, normally I would have smoked a cigarette now!" Also, don't avoid public places. Just go out and live your life! You have just regained total freedom, you have something to celebrate, and you have something to share.

Share your experience with other smokers. Help them to become free, happy nonsmokers. Share your thoughts with them. Advise them to read this book. Buy them a copy of this book, or just give them your copy. Don't laugh at other smokers or become angry with them. Always respect them and try to help them if they want to be helped. Don't force them into anything. You know that this wouldn't work.

Finally, experience your Final Liberation and live free, happy, and healthy!!

I'm proud of you!

You can be proud of yourself!

Best wishes,

Eric Eraly

22. 365 days after Final Liberation (read this chapter after your Final Liberation is a fact)

I bet you all wish you could already say that you have been free from smoking for 365 days right now. This is not the case, since we can't change time.

You know that this day will come. You know that soon enough, you'll be able to say that you have been a free, happy nonsmoker for a year. Then two years will follow, three years, and so on. The reason why you are so sure about it is that, due to your Final Liberation, you have absolutely no more desire for a cigarette. You can easily see through all the illusions and beliefs you had about smoking. You know very well that cigarettes give you no benefits or pleasure at all. These were illusions created in your body and mind by the nicotine balloon effect and heterosuggestions from the world around you.

The journey you have made was a very exciting journey. I think you'll agree with me, won't you? Now, the new journey you are about to start will be a very exciting one. It will be a journey of new discoveries, new ways of life, and a new personality. You'll discover so many new things. The things you used to do in the past will have new meaning. Your participation in social events will become different and more intense. The people around you will approach you differently. You'll have another view on the world around you. It will be a very beautiful and amazing adventure, full of joy, energy, and lust for life.

As our journey is ending, I would like to ask you a favor, my dear friend and free, happy nonsmoker. I would like to know your story. I am curious about the adventure you are about to begin. It's not only me, but thousands and thousands of people who would like to know the details of your adventure.

I would appreciate it if you could write a few pages about the things you experienced during your first year after becoming a free, happy nonsmoker.

Since you are probably in the habit of using a journal, you could continue it for a while and send me a copy. You can send us your story by e-mail at support@PainlessStopSmokingCure.com.

Or you can leave your feedback and comments at our blog: www.PainlessStopSmokingCure.com/blog.

Through these messages, I wish to share the message with other smokers about how to improve their way of living by freeing themselves from nicotine. I hope that this book will help more people to take that easy step and join us on this wonderful adventure, which is called "life."

I want to congratulate you for your splendid work over the recent hours. I'm sure you'll enjoy life much more as a free, happy nonsmoker. I also want to thank you for sharing your new adventure with the world.

Take care!

Enjoy, and…take a deep breath! (Now you can!)

MORE INPUT AND BONUS :

When you are looking for more input and coaching, or when you want to advocate the Painless Stop Smoking Cure to your friends and colleagues and earn *significant bonuses* by helping other smokers to become smoke-free, check out our website and blog at:

www.PainlessStopSmokingCure.com

www.PainlessStopSmokingCure.com/blog

www.PainlessStopSmokingCure.com/affiliate